THE NEW MERMAIDS

The Playboy of the Western World

THE NEW MERMAIDS

General Editors

BRIAN MORRIS
Professor of English Literature, University of Sheffield

BRIAN GIBBONS
Lecturer in English, University of York

ROMA GILL
Senior Lecturer in English Literature, University of Sheffield

The Playboy of the Western World

—∿∿∿∿⊙∿∿∿∿—

JOHN MILLINGTON SYNGE

Edited by MALCOLM KELSALL

Lecturer in English
University of Reading

ERNEST BENN LIMITED
LONDON & TONBRIDGE

First published in this form 1975
by Ernest Benn Limited
25 New Street Square Fleet Street London EC4A 3JA
& Sovereign Way Tonbridge Kent TN9 1RW

© *Ernest Benn Limited 1975*

Distributed in Canada by
The General Publishing Company Limited Toronto

Printed in Great Britain

ISBN 0 510-33771-6 *Paperback*

CONTENTS

ACKNOWLEDGEMENTS

IN EDITING the text I have made much use of the Oxford edition of the *Collected Works* of J. M. Synge edited by Robin Skelton, Alan Price, and Ann Saddlemyer (1962–68), referred to hereafter as *Works*, which makes available a substantial quantity of MS material. The reader interested in the imaginative genesis of *The Playboy* should consult the fourth volume of this edition. My research has been aided by the generous financial assistance of the Research Board of Reading University, and the publishers of the New Mermaids. Among many individuals I should like to thank particularly Professor Malcolm Brown, Dr Joan Byrne, Dr Ian Fletcher, Miss M. F. MacNally, curator of Thoor Ballylee, Mr D. T. O'Rourke, son of the original 'Philly Cullen', and in general the staff of the National Library in Dublin and of Trinity College Library whose prompt helpfulness at all times added to the pleasure of visiting Ireland. My greatest debt is due to my wife Mary, without whose assistance in preparing the text it would not now have appeared.

The song 'John McGoldrick and the Quaker's Daughter' (from *Irish Street Ballads*, collected by Colm O Lochlainn) is reproduced by permission of The Three Candles Limited, Dublin.

Reading   M.M.K.
September 1973

INTRODUCTION

THE AUTHOR

EDMUND JOHN MILLINGTON SYNGE was born in Newtown Villas, Rathfarnham near Dublin on 16 April 1871.[1] The family were land-owners and Protestant, of the declining Ascendancy class. Synge's father, a barrister, died in the following year, but left adequate means for the support of his family; Synge's mother, the daughter of an enthusiastic Protestant clergyman, Robert Traill, survived until 1908. It is reported that she never attended a performance of any of her son's plays.

Synge graduated 'passed in the second class' from Trinity College, Dublin in 1892, the year of the founding of the Irish Literary Society in Dublin, and two years after the fall of Parnell. His interests at this time were primarily linguistic (he had studied German, Hebrew, and Irish) and musical, and the following year, persuaded by his cousin Mary Synge, a concert pianist, he left for Germany to pursue his musical studies. In the same year the Gaelic League was founded. By 1895 he had abandoned music and was studying French at the Sorbonne; in 1896 he visited Italy. Relations with his family were strained because he had broken with Christianity; early private tuition and long periods of solitary study fostered the inward-looking meditativeness which Yeats commemorates; there was a series of hopeless romantic entanglements with women. Under no necessity of making a choice of life, he was unable to discover a vocation.

In Paris he met a then minor bard of the Celtic twilight and a young feminist political agitator. He was present with W. B. Yeats and Maud Gonne at the inaugural meeting of the Irish League (*L'Association Irlandaise*) on 1 January 1897, but shortly resigned (6 April).

[1] I am indebted to David H. Greene and Edward M. Stephens, *J. M. Synge* (New York, 1959).

Yeats claimed that Synge 'seemed by nature unfitted to think a political thought',[2] and it appears that the creator of Christy Mahon was no friend of nationalistic violence. It was Yeats, whom Synge had met for the first time on 21 December 1896, who gave him the now famous advice to visit the Aran Islands. 'Give up Paris. You will never create anything by reading Racine, and Arthur Symons will always be a better critic of French literature. Go to the Aran Islands. Live there as if you were one of the people themselves; express a life that has never found expression' – such is Yeats's recollection recorded in the Preface to *The Well of the Saints* in 1905.

The advice was neglected for a time while Synge pursued his current interests in Breton folklore, and the first visit to the Aran Islands was not made until May 1898. He was to come back repeatedly to the west coast, returning in the four succeeding summers to the islands, and in 1905 travelling with Jack Yeats through the Congested Districts further north on a commission from the *Manchester Guardian*. Although as a writer in the summer of 1898 he found his subject, he had yet to find an audience. The manuscript of *The Aran Islands* was regularly rejected by publishers, and did not appear until 1907 when it was issued, with illustrations by Jack Yeats, by Elkin Mathews in London and Maunsel & Co. in Dublin. Meantime the first play of Synge's to be performed was *The Shadow of the Glen* in 1903, put on by the Irish National Theatre Society in the inadequacies of the Molesworth Hall, Dublin, and published in Yeats's *Samhain* 4 (December 1904), and simultaneously in New York by John Quinn.

Synge by this time had become actively concerned with the National Theatre movement which had grown from the Irish Literary Theatre of 1899 and which was to acquire a permanent home in 1904 at the Abbey Theatre thanks to the generosity of Miss A. E. F. Horniman. Synge, Lady Gregory, and Yeats became the directors of a professionalized company in 1905. *Riders to the Sea* had already gone on at the Molesworth Hall in 1904, having previously appeared in *Samhain* 3 (1903), and was issued together with *The Shadow of the Glen* by Elkin Mathews in 1905. Synge's first play produced at the Abbey was *The Well of the Saints* in 1905, the last (in his lifetime)

[2] *Essays and Introductions* (1961), p. 319.

The Playboy of the Western World in 1907, which opened on Saturday 26 January, and survived the execrations of Irish patriotism and purity until the end of the following week thanks to the exertions of the police, and the testimonies in court by Yeats against the rioters.

The last two years of Synge's life were passed in growing sickness under the attacks of Hodgkin's Disease, for which an operation had been performed in 1897. He was engaged to the young Molly Allgood ('Maire O'Neill'), who first played Pegeen, but the marriage did not take place. His intimate letters to her are now available for the morbidly curious.[3] *The Tinker's Wedding*, 'too dangerous to put on in the Abbey' Synge wrote, was published by Maunsel & Co. (1907), his *Poems and Translations* appeared posthumously in the year of his death, 1909. *Deidre of the Sorrows*, on which he was working when he died, was first produced at the Abbey in 1910 with Molly Allgood in the title role.

THE PLAY

There is no need to tell again the story of *The Playboy* riots. A work which seemed to represent the Irish as violent and superstitious, blatherers, braggarts, sots, and above all obscene, was not likely to recommend itself to nationalistic sentiment. *The Shadow of the Glen* had already fallen foul of Arthur Griffith[4] and that penwoman of bloodthirsty dramatic tableaux, Maud Gonne, and, if William Fay's memory is correct, Synge was looking for trouble.[5] A major clash between the Abbey and the nationalists had always been probable. The police had been called to protect the first night of the first play of the dramatic movement, Yeats's *The Countess Cathleen* (1899), which smelt of blasphemy to some. The Abbey was financed by an English sponsor. The directors were of the Protestant Ascendancy, and sometimes overt in their sense of superiority to the Dublin

[3] *Letters to Molly: John M. Synge to Maire O'Neill*, ed. Ann Saddlemyer (Cambridge, Mass., 1971).
[4] Editor of the *United Irishman*, and founder of Sinn Fein.
[5] W. G. Fay and Catherine Carswell, *The Fays of the Abbey Theatre* (1935), pp. 211f.

middle classes. Obstinate in obtaining their ends, they had quarrelled not only with the public, but with their fellows in the theatre. But the Irish dramatic movement throve on controversy. It is good publicity.

The Playboy is in many ways the finest embodiment of the early ideals of the movement, and the Abbey Company closed ranks round Synge. On the other hand, even as Synge's work embodies those ideals, it changes, and even subverts or mocks them. If this can be recognized, then some, at least, of the early antagonism to the work is not as absurd as commonly viewed. William Fay was distressed by Synge's bitterness.[6] Lady Gregory, though she fought tirelessly for *The Playboy*, confessed to Hugh Lane that she hated it.[7] Yeats, in the organ of the movement, *Samhain*, often seems cast in the role of a critical John the Baptist proclaiming the coming of a Messiah (who is John Synge), but Synge did not praise Yeats's work, so the poet comments, probably because he would not flatter,[8] and the kind of drama that Synge created is of a different world than the coterie art of aristocratic salons of which Yeats dreams in *A People's Theatre*.

Yeats claimed, nonetheless, that Synge was a creation of the dramatic movement. What he has in common with the Abbey must be established before the individuality of his satiric comedy can be justly seen. It was the aim of the movement to express the national spirit by turning 'To the people'[9] and to whatever was 'ancient, or simple, or noble' in Ireland.[10] The life and imagination of the folk, the history, legends, and myths of the land: these were the staple of theatrical creation. Two ideals difficult to reconcile inspired the Abbey: a desire for realism, and a desire for poetic beauty. At times the ideals diverge into the sub-Ibsenesque and the superhuman: Moore and Yeats, but their potential creative fusion is a *leitmotiv* of Yeats's theatrical criticism. A truly national theatre, furthermore, would be free from local political concerns. The directors were unanimous on

---

[6] ibid.

[7] Quoted by Elizabeth Coxhead, *Lady Gregory, a Literary Portrait* (2nd edn. 1966) p. 117.

[8] Coxhead, op. cit., p. 111 discusses the issue, and thinks it a fair inference that Synge did not like Yeats's plays.

[9] *Explorations* (1962), p. 83.

[10] ibid., p. 136.

that. What Yeats desired was a drama that would be as intellectually liberating as that of Athens or Elizabethan London, in which individual energy might display itself with an intensity transcending mere social utility and commonplace generality. Hence the defence of *The Playboy* involved the fundamental principles of the theatre. Finally, the argument against parochial nationalism was carried further. A great Irish writer would be cosmopolitan in his culture. He would have to be so because there was no Irish theatrical tradition of merit on which he could draw, and because the truths of art are universal. 'All literature in every country is derived from models, and as often as not these are foreign models', wrote Yeats, and adds, 'it is the presence of a personal element alone that can give it nationality in a fine sense, the nationality of its maker.'[11]

Clearly Synge fulfils these Yeatsian ideals in general. He was conversant with the best that had been thought and said in many lands, but drew his immediate inspiration from the common people of his own country. His plays were not directed to social or political ends, but are the work of a man who is both a realist and a poet, who sought not only beauty of language, but suggested too in his stories the presence of half-remembered archetypal tales and ancient myths. The relation between Synge and Yeats, however, has been often elaborated, while Synge's relationship with his fellow workers at the Abbey has been correspondingly passed over, in part because of the persuasive enchantment of the propagandist rhetoric of Yeats. The poet drew a picture of Synge as a solitary genius within the dramatic movement, undergoing an almost religious transformation in the Aran Islands,[12] and then, like Parnell, falling as another victim to the middle-class Irish pack. Thus, in Synge's development, the contribution has been neglected of Edward Martyn's mystical treatment of Nature, of the satire and farce of William Boyle and Lady Gregory, Padraic Colum's fusion of the heroic with peasant naturalism, and even of the importance of the player for whom Synge created the role of Christy Mahon,

[11] ibid., p. 233.
[12] *A Vision* (1962), p. 167. 'He had to undergo an aesthetic transformation, analogous to religious conversion, before he became the audacious, joyous, ironical man we know.'

comic actor of genius, producer and stage-manager, and Lord High
Everythingelse: William Fay. But Fay was not smart enough to be
invited to Coole Park.

The realism of *The Playboy* derives directly from the Abbey tradition of the 'peasant play.' The movement 'To the people' was not
intended to be sentimental, but aimed to replace the 'stage Irishman'
of a decadent tradition with the real language and passion of men.
Hence the importance for Synge, as for the company, that the setting of
The Playboy, the language, the actions of the characters, should be
grounded in recognizable fact. Thus we have the concern of the Abbey
with correctness of costume and cottage setting which Frank Fay
emphasizes and William Fay recalls with mathematical detail. So
too Synge insists that his dialogue is based on real speech he has
overheard, leading thus to his unfortunate story of listening through
a chink in the floor in Wicklow. The action of the play is based on two
authentic stories of outlaws shielded by the people of the west, one a
father-murderer, Synge believed, sheltered on Inishmaan,[13] the other,
James Lynchehaun, a nationalist hero.[14] The action of *The Playboy*,
Synge argued, was at least true to the 'psychic state' of the locality.[15]

This realistic foundation, however, sustains an extravaganza so
wild that it subverts everything on which it is grounded. The naturalism
of the setting is merely a foil to the wild imagination of the peasants
which rises to fantastic absurdity: witness the mad logic of the argu-

[13] *Works*, II, 95, reports the tale of 'a Connaught man who killed his father
with the blow of a spade when he was in a passion, and then fled to this island
and threw himself on the mercy of some of the natives with whom he was
said to be related. They hid him ... and kept him safe for weeks ... In
spite of a reward which was offered, the island was incorruptible, and after
much trouble the man was safely shipped to America'. Yeats had heard the
story, *Autobiographies* (1961), p. 569, and Arthur Symons and Thomas
Johnson Westropp, the antiquarian, also report it; see Greene and Stephens,
op. cit., n. 37 & n. 38. Tomás O'Máille, *An Ghaoth Aniar* (Dublin 1920),
pp. 93–8, traces the original of the story, and reports that the father was not
killed.
[14] Lynchehaun assaulted a woman on Achill Island, but was sheltered from
the police and eventually escaped to the U.S.A. The courts refused to ex-
tradite him on the grounds that he was a political refugee. His name is
mentioned by Synge in a draft of *The Playboy*.
[15] Letter to Stephen MacKenna, quoted in Greene and Stephens, op. cit.,
p. 265.

ment that a parricide is a good potboy. The language of the people moves to laughter by its very bizarreness (to employ a Beckettian term) as much as it rouses admiration by its imaginative richness: Old Mahon's 'Is my visage astray?' (III, 185–6) is pure Mrs Rooney. Finally, what could be more gross than Synge's handling of the tale of the murderer which is told so differently in *The Aran Islands*? There it is illustrative of a pagan and sympathetic code of conduct alien to the English law.[16] The outlaw belongs to the people because a crime of tragic passion is outside the jurisdiction of a mechanical and foreign legalism. (It is easy to see, thus, how Christy's other real-life prototype, Lynchehaun, became a nationalist hero.) But what was dignified in the prose (and possibly influenced in Synge's telling by William Morris's *News from Nowhere*) becomes not only farce in *The Playboy*, but also bloody and intentionally disgusting. It is bad enough not to have killed your father once, but to fail to do it three times is to reduce what has been described as an Oedipean act, or quasi-Frazerian ritual, to rollicking pantomine. Yet Old Mahon is plastered in the blood of the naturalistic theatre, as Colum records,[17] and when he scrabbles on his knees towards an equally scrabbling Christy, just burnt with shocking viciousness by a lighted turf sod, to be greeted by the cry of one astonished by the absurdity and cruelty of the world: 'Are you coming to be killed a third time, or what ails you now?' (III, 594–5) – then there would seem to be only two natural

[16] 'This impulse to protect the criminal is universal in the west. It seems partly due to the association between justice and the hated English jurisdiction, but more directly to the primitive feeling of these people, who are never criminals yet always capable of crime, that a man will not do wrong unless he is under the influence of a passion which is as irresponsible as a storm on the sea. If a man has killed his father, and is already sick and broken with remorse, they can see no reason why he should be dragged away and killed by the law.

'Such a man, they say, will be quiet all the rest of his life, and if you suggest that punishment is needed as an example, they ask, "Would any one kill his father if he was able to help it?" ' *Works*, II, 95.

[17] 'That scene was too representational. There stood a man with horribly-bloodied bandage upon his head, making a figure that took the whole thing out of the atmosphere of high comedy'. *The Road Round Ireland* (New York, 1926), p. 368. Cyril Cusack also comments that the naturalism of the early Abbey tradition worked against the enjoyment of *The Playboy*, 'A Player's Reflections on *Playboy*', *Modern Drama*, IV (1961), 300–5.

reactions for an audience, and there goes only a pair of shears between them, outraged disgust, or the cathartic release of shock through laughter. Synge, after all, is the compatriot of Swift.

A representation of the latent violence of Irish society by the Abbey did not have to wait upon Synge, nor were comic satire and ridicule new to the movement (as the popular success of Boyle shows), but Synge's peasant comedy is sharper to the taste and less easy to digest than the work of his predecessors. Boyle, for instance, withdrew his works in protest. The point may be readily illustrated by reference to the farces of Lady Gregory. The situation of *The Playboy* is already present in *Spreading the News*, the action of which depends upon a village's love of gossip and what Colum calls 'ideal' violence, leading to a harmless attempt to return a hayfork being magnified to a pursuit, a quarrel, a murder from sexual motives, and the arrest of the protagonists. 'I suppose there is a good deal of disorder in this place?' a Magistrate asks at the beginning, and runs rapidly through common assault to agrarian crime and thence, by an easy progression, to murder. Likewise, the character of Christy is foreshadowed in the eponymous hero of *Hyacinth Halvey*, a bashful and feeble young man but represented by his testimonials as possessing 'the fire of the Gael, the strength of the Norman, the vigour of the Dane, the stolidity of the Saxon'. But there were no riots when Hyacinth proclaimed, 'I will break the law. Drunk or sober I'll break it. I'll do something that will have no excuse. What would you say is the worst crime that any man can do?' But the reason why Lady Gregory aroused no protest may be readily seen if one compares an extended passage from her work with Synge. Here is the climax of violence from *Spreading the News* set against *The Playboy*. Jack Smith, supposedly murdered, tries to get at Bartley, his 'murderer' who is 'eloping' with Jack's wife:

JACK SMITH
    Let me at him till I break his head!

    BARTLEY *backs in terror. Neighbours hold* JACK SMITH *back (trying to free himself)*
    Let me at him! Isn't he the pleasant sort of a scarecrow for any woman to be crossing the ocean with! It's back from the docks of New York he'd be turned (*trying to rush at him again*), with a lie in his mouth and treachery in his heart, and another man's

wife by his side, and he passing her off as his own! Let me at him, can't you.

> *Makes another rush, but is held back*

MAGISTRATE (*pointing to* JACK SMITH)

Policeman, put the handcuffs on this man. I see it all now. A case of false impersonation, a conspiracy to defeat the ends of justice. There was a case in the Andaman Islands, a murderer of the Mopsa tribe, a religious enthusiast –

*   *   *

> (CHRISTY) *squirms round on the floor and bites* SHAWN's *leg*

SHAWN (*shrieking*)

My leg's bit on me! He's the like of a mad dog, I'm thinking, the way that I will surely die.

CHRISTY (*delighted with himself*)

You will then, the way you can shake out hell's flags of welcome for my coming in two weeks or three, for I'm thinking Satan hasn't many have killed their da in Kerry, and in Mayo too.

> *Old* MAHON *comes in behind on all fours and looks on unnoticed*

MEN (*to* PEGEEN)

Bring the sod, will you.

PEGEEN (*coming over*)

God help him so. (*Burns his leg*)

CHRISTY (*kicking and screaming*)

Oh, glory be to God!   (III, 583–92)

In Lady Gregory it is clear that Jack Smith, held back by the neighbours, is not going to be able to harm anyone, nor would anyone harm him. His creator has put him in handcuffs before the policeman does so, and someone soon will be able to explain all the mistakes of the action and all will end well. The Magistrate, although a duffer who understands nothing of what is going on, is nonetheless a buffer preventing a collision and represents the forces of law and order which, if the subject of comedy like Elbow and his like, are yet generally accepted by the audience. Lady Gregory's farces are the bloodless *jeux d'esprit* of aristocratic superiority. Her peasants in the plays merely romp with picturesque liveliness (unless lamenting, as in *The Gaol Gate*, in a charming Kiltartan parody of the language of the Authorized Version).

In Synge, on the other hand, violence which has been merely the subject of gossip, now intrudes with total brutality before our eyes. Shawn's cry may be partially comic, Christy's is not. Pegeen's act loses all dramatic significance if she does not wish to hurt the man who has humiliated her. What is more, the cry is rank blasphemy, and comes from the lips of one who has proclaimed himself a hero of hell, now burnt by retributive fire. At the same time Old Mahon's entry, as if instantly propelled by Christy's yet again false boast of having killed him, is a Jonsonian comic climax achieved by the simple means of ever speeding up the farcical action. Thus the audience is led simultaneously to mutually irreconcilable reactions. The actors must play both with convincing naturalism, and at the same time with a buoyant sense of wild comic extravagance, and it is this compressed complexity which distinguishes the art of Synge from the charming dilettantism of Lady Gregory.

Possibly Synge's achievement might be seen as enriching his sources rather than subverting them, were he not so deliberately provocative. There can be little doubt that he set himself throughout *The Playboy* to play merry hell with the 'ancient idealism' of Ireland which it was the self-declared intention of the Abbey to foster,[18] and which Abbey comedy and satire never attacks. In so doing he is, in some measure, reverting to an older Irish tradition as Vivien Mercier suggests,[19] in which even the greatest heroes of legend or myth are treated with macabre or grotesque humour. As a Gaelic speaker he would know the pungency and obscenity of the old tales which are as far from the golden glimmerings of a Celtic twilight as is *The Playboy* from the romantic and myth-creating poetic vision of Synge's own apprehension in the Aran Islands of the simple and wild human heart among the beauty and terror of the permanent forms and forces of Nature. Ann Saddlemyer has noted the tendency to self-parody in Synge.[20] It is a Byronic

[18] 'Synge . . . takes a malicious pleasure in the contrast between his hero, whom he discovers through his instinct for comedy, and any hero in men's minds . . . he is ready to sacrifice every convention, perhaps all that men have agreed to reverence, for a startling theme'. Yeats, *A Vision*, p. 165.

[19] *The Irish Comic Tradition* (Oxford, 1962). Mercier argues that *The Playboy* negates many of the values of the Literary Revival, pp. 247–8.

[20] *J. M. Synge and Modern Comedy* (Dublin, 1968). She suggests that Synge's desire to experiment would have driven him away from the Abbey.

quality, and there is a case for claiming that *The Playboy* stands to *The Aran Islands* as *Don Juan* to *Childe Harold*.

A representative play from the dramatic movement may illustrate some of the motifs of Irish idealism which Synge brutally humorizes. Padraic Colum's powerful work *The Fiddler's House* (originally *Broken Soil*) is among the finest of the early plays of the literary revival, though Colum, like Boyle, broke with the Abbey. The protagonist, Conn Hourican, like Christie of Lady Gregory's *Twenty Five* or Synge's tramp in *The Shadow of the Glen*, is a celebrant of freedom. He longs for the open road. He seeks too the competition and company of his fellow musicians, a longing which even a student for the priest-hood, Justin Reilly, cannot deny. Like the Jacobites, whose songs Conn loves, it is 'always before him to win something', and in dream-ing of winning 'something grander and finer' than what he now pos-sesses, he shows a romantic imagination of the same order as that of the heroes of Synge. Of equal importance to the story of Conn is that of the unavailing struggle of Brian McConnell to subject Conn's daughter, Maire, to marriage. Just as Conn is the descendant of the minstrels of old, so Brian is of the blood of ancient heroes 'with the strong hand and the wild heart', of a family of violent men, a tamer of horses, who seems as if by the force of will and body to bring every-thing within his grip. But Maire chooses the freedom of the road, and the farm passes into the keeping of the gentler sister Anne and the sentimental versifier James Moynihan. The play is suffused with the spirit of song and of poetry, and the legendary past and natural peasant life are finely blended with a positive force and emotive sin-cerity intended to quicken the spirit of what Colum sees as the true Ireland. Here, close to the soil, is a land of poets and heroic fighters, not without faults, insouciant, passionate, unruly, but respectful of religion and lovers of things that are fine and free.

Compare with Colum's treatment of poetry, Synge's Michael drunkenly bellowing a nationalistic melody as he staggers home from the 'funferall'. Michael is merely sottish, and Synge is pointing for-ward to the satire of O'Casey. Likewise compare the respectful but independent attitude of Colum's peasants to Justin Reilly with the gibbering of Shawn about Father Reilly: 'but I'm afeard of Father

Reilly; and what at all would the Holy Father and the Cardinals of Rome be saying . . .?' (I, 110–12). Conn Hourican quits security for the open road because he wishes to win the prize of the Feis of Ardagh, and longs to be a chief minstrel of Ireland. Christy's poetry, on the other hand, is a compound of romantic lies. Brian would lead men with the same power as he breaks horses. Christy's highest equinine feat is on a mule; his heroic deed a bang on the head, to no avail, with a spade. Here is his heroic vision when he masters his father; 'Go with you, is it? I will then, like a gallant captain with his heathen slave. Go on now and I'll see you from this day stewing my oatmeal and washing my spuds, for I'm master of all fights from now. (*Pushing* MAHON) Go on, I'm saying' (III, 607–10). Clearly this is burlesque, although, at times, by the power of language *The Playboy* rises to the ambiguities of mock-heroic.

Synge was not merely mocking heroic Ireland. Christy is a hero of European literary type, something of a Plautian or Jonsonian *miles gloriosus*, but a 'humour' character who defeats expectation by actually becoming what he pretended to be. The manuscripts show that Rabelais was running in Synge's mind, and Christy has something of the vulgar energy of Panurge, but there is a hint too of Don Quixote. Modern criticism[21] has been eager to suggest other heroic or mythic analogues, although a sceptical mind may find the list a little long: Saturn and Zeus, Prometheus and Parnell, Ossian and Beowulf, Dionysus and Jesse James, Oedipus (Christy does not kill his father, and is asked to marry a woman old enough to be his mother), and, above all, by substituting an ass for a mule and dropping a 'y', an even more remarkable parallel has been observed.

To pursue merely heroic analogues: as an heroic type Mahon's looney possesses certain essential qualities. He is mighty of strength. Did he not cleave his father to an assortment of depths by letting fall a loy on his skull? He is a winner of all chivalric sports, on foot or on mule-back. He is a man too of sudden violence like Achilles or the

[21] There is an extensive bibliography in S. B. Bushrui ed., *Sunshine and the Moon's Delight* (Gerrards Cross and Beirut, 1972), pp. 317–38. This volume contains 'A Survey of Recent Work on J. M. Synge' by Alan Price, pp. 279–95, which updates the critical introduction to Price's *Synge and Anglo-Irish Drama* (1961).

'angry boy' Cuchulain. The loy, obviously, is the weapon of the hero, his Excalibur or *gae Bulga*, well known to fame, while enthusiasts of the phallus and the trinity of Frazer, Freud, and Frye, will find their own meaning in the moment when the lowered loy is riz. Pegeen plays Delilah to this bound Irish Samson. Pursuing this Joycean sport a little further, it is not beyond the bounds of possibility that there are further overtones in the scene where the Mayo girls bring Christy food. Voracious appetite for food and women characterizes several Irish heroes (and Panurge), and the scene in which the drift of Mayo women partake of a feast where more than culinary delights are on offer, may have more than one literary antecedent. Add to this the constant allusions to the Bible and the Church with which Synge's characters lard their discourse, and one may readily become hag-ridden with the Joycean spirit. But this is merely scratching the surface, for the theme of the play, the rebellion of youth against age, son against father, is at the root of Western civilization. Are we not all sons of Adam? Or if this does not take the line far enough back, there is a greater rebel yet. One of the many meanings of 'playboy' in popular use is, quite simply, 'the devil'.[22]

It is in keeping both with Synge's interests, and the ideals of the literary revivalists, that traditional legend and myth should be seen behind a modern tale. Nonetheless analogy is not the same as allusion, nor does allusion imply the existence of a sustained referential scheme. If this were not so, anything might mean everything. *The Playboy* is not like *Ulysses*. It is transparently obvious in narrative line; its basic parody of heroic motifs does not work to a sustained scheme like *Ulysses*, nor even by the method of allusion of a work like *Don Quixote*; while the frequent religious references are usually merely blasphemous in that they tie sacred things to things profane, or reduce them to mere absurdity, witness Michael's wish that Christy should throw his dead father 'on the crupper of a Kerry mule and drive him westwards, like holy Joseph in the days gone by' (III, 323–4). Synge is a

[22] The senses of the word are examined by Maurice Bourgeois, *John Millington Synge and the Irish Theatre* (1913), pp. 193–4 n. A tripartite division is made: (*a*) one who is played with; (*b*) one who plays like a player, either as comedian or athletic champion; (*c*) one who is full of the play spirit, a wild dare-devil.

learned writer, but his aim was simplicity, to digest wide reading into an art which common men might relish – had not Shakespeare and Molière done the same? – and hence the tendency of Synge's work is opposed to that of Joyce and the pedantically pretentious obscurantism of modernism.

The difficulty of Synge's work is not in discovering hidden meanings – even the shifting senses of the word 'playboy' are always obvious in context – but in determining its tone and the validity of its style. How seriously is one to take the celebration of irresponsibility, sexuality, and brutality in Synge? When Christy awakens and finds his dream true and has become the hero his poetic imagination conceived, how serious an ideal does this represent? Fundamentally, for everything depends on it, what are we to make of the language? Is it truly poetic? Burlesque and mock-heroic? Pretentious verbiage? Criticism has, on the whole, shirked the question which, in the theatre, must be asked at the beginning: how are the lines to be said? For how they are said determines the way in which their meaning is assessed.

Consider Synge first as 'the evil genius of the Abbey',[23] the man, in his own phrase, of 'Satanic or barbarous sympathies',[24] who linked comedy with the powers of darkness:

> Of the things which nourish the imagination humour is one of the most needful, and it is dangerous to limit or destroy it. Baudelaire calls laughter the greatest sign of the Satanic element in man; and where a country loses its humour, as some towns in Ireland are doing, there will be morbidity of mind, as Baudelaire's mind was morbid. (Preface to *The Tinker's Wedding*)

The Satanic reference points the way back to that 'School of Poetry' which Southey attacked and of which Synge is a late offspring. He is at one with Blake, Byron, and Shelley and that whole romantic movement which rebelled against established religion and society, and violent of imagination, or outrageous of life, created images of supermen:

[23] For Holloway's views on *The Playboy* see *Joseph Holloway's Abbey Theatre*, ed. Robert Hogan and Michael J. O'Neill (Carbondale, Illinois, 1967), pp. 81–8 passim.

[24] 'The man who feels most exquisitely the joy of contact with what is perfect in art and nature is the man who from the width and power of his thought hides the greatest number of Satanic or barbarous sympathies'. *Works*, II, 6.

Los, the sun of poetry, Prometheus the fire-giver, Don Juan sailing on the ocean of woman. More locally one thinks of Yeats attacking the empty morality of the newspaper or market place and demanding an art that is 'beating against the walls of the world',[25] that gives imaginative delight because of its intense abundance, not on account of its utility: 'when Lucifer stands among his friends, when Villon sings his dead ladies to so gallant a rhythm, when Timon makes his epitaph, we feel no sorrow, for life herself has made one of her eternal gestures, has called up into our hearts her energy that is eternal delight'.[26] Here Blake and Yeats join hands across the nineteenth century.

It is certain that Synge, like Yeats, wished to shock that 'ungodly ruck of fat-faced sweaty-headed swine':[27] Catholic Dublin. Possibly his Satanism is even pathological, springing from his adolescent rebellion against Christianity: thus the tying of a cleric in a sack and his humiliation in *The Tinker's Wedding*, or the desire to write a play in which rape is the preferred alternative to a Catholic and Protestant sheltering together. His reference to the sexual longings of the unsatisfied saints in heaven (in *The Playboy*) shows a similar demonic mischievousness.

Yet although Synge is the heir of the dark rebels of romanticism, like Byron he finds hell an amusing place. Because he is a comic writer it is difficult to place him seriously alongside Nietzsche, Lawrence, or Yeats, witness the entry of that imp of Satan, Christy, which establishes the comic norm of *The Playboy*: Shawn, in all the terror of stage cowardice, bursts in, 'God help me, he's following me now, and if he's heard what I said, he'll be having my life, and I going home lonesome in the darkness of the night' (I, 151–3). *Parturiunt montes, nascitur ridiculus mus*. Shawn does not need God's help against this terror that walks by night, who now creeps in, slight, tired, dirty, and frightened, as much an object of curiosity as of fear to the rest of the household, and the first words of the parricide are, of course, a model of religious propriety: 'God save all here!' (I, 154). Synge is complaining of Ireland as Byron complained of his times: 'I want a hero'. Europe's

[25] *Explorations*, p. 193.
[26] ibid., p. 163.
[27] Synge, letter to Stephen MacKenna, quoted in Greene and Stephens, op. cit., p. 264.

great men did not satisfy Byron the would-be epic poet, who states therefore,

> Of such as these I should not care to vaunt,
> I'll therefore take our ancient friend Don Juan –
> We all have seen him, in the pantomime,
> Sent to the devil somewhat ere his time.

Likewise, in an Ireland of plaster saints, Father Reillys, and Shaneens, Synge offers the pantomime imp, Mahon's looney. The bathotic device employed in Christy's entry is the foundation of the entire action of the play which, with classic economy, is built merely on varying this incident. Every time Christy rises higher it is to fall lower. The confrontation with Old Mahon, whom we are not surprised to find still lives, is inevitable, just as we know that Subtle and Face in *The Alchemist* cannot keep up their deceptions forever, and the comic bubble is stretched to ever greater limits of absurdity until it bursts. Synge's break with tradition is merely to make his *miles gloriosus* brave, as if Falstaff should slim and become courageous, and by substituting violent naturalism for comic fantasy at the end of the action he achieves a striking reversal of tone. He thought, so he wrote, of Alceste or of Shylock and of their ambivalence.[28] A change of mood does not necessarily imply a change of philosophical outlook, however, and aesthetic considerations of variety and climax may have determined the presentation of Christy as master of all fights, rather than the desire to present Satanism seriously.

Criticism has often debated the point, and, at least, it is widely agreed that contradictory elements are fused together in Synge's work. Especial emphasis has been given to the interplay between

---

[28] ' "The Playboy of the Western World" is not a play with "a purpose" in the modern sense of the word, but although parts of it are, or are meant to be, extravagant comedy, still a great deal that is in it, and a great deal more that is behind it, is perfectly serious, when looked at in a certain light. That is often the case, I think, with comedy, and no one is quite sure to-day whether "Shylock" and "Alceste" should be played seriously or not. There are, it may be hinted, several sides to "The Playboy" .' From Synge's letter in the *Irish Times*, 31 January 1907, in James Kilroy, *The 'Playboy' Riots* (Dublin, 1971), pp. 40–1.

'dream' and 'reality' in *The Playboy*, and it is evident at the end of the work that Christy's false dream of himself has become true. How seriously this should be taken, however, is a nice point. The collision between dream and reality is basic to all burlesque and mock-heroic writing. In the first, low deeds in low language provide a monstrous parody of heroic values. Thus, the 'murder' of Old Mahon provokes the following Homeric simile: 'You never hanged him, the way Jimmy Farrell hanged his dog from the licence, and had it screeching and wriggling three hours at the butt of a string, and himself swearing it was a dead dog, and the peelers swearing it had life?' (I, 251–4). In the mock-heroic low things ('reality') are celebrated in the lofty language of 'dream', for example: 'How would a lovely handsome woman the like of you be lonesome when all men should be thronging around to hear the sweetness of your voice, and the little infant children should be pestering your steps I'm thinking, and you walking the roads' (II, 248–52). This is fine writing, as parts of *The Rape of the Lock* are high poetry divorced from context, but we are not allowed to forget that context. The Widow Quin, like the eloquent Dempsey's wife,[29] always sees through a playboy's rhetoric: 'There's poetry talk for a girl you'd see itching and scratching, and she with a stale stink of poteen on her from selling in the shop' (II, 496–6). Mock-heroic has been judged as superior to burlesque because it blends grandeur of language with satiric ridicule, but its ultimate tendency is always to move laughter by ridicule, and laughter, Hobbes claimed, is the product of that sudden glory in which we perceive our superiority to those we laugh at. Pegeen is no Cathleen ni Houlihan. It is inconceivable that Maud Gonne would play the role. *The Playboy*, classic in its form and stylistic devices, is classic too in its content. It deals with low people, and ridicules follies below the scope of tragedy.

Pegeen is given a speech that makes the point clear. 'I'll say, a strange man is a marvel, with his mighty talk; but what's a squabble in your back-yard, and the blow of a loy, have taught me that there's a great

[29] The eponymous hero of Boyle's play, a hypocritical rhetorician, referred to as a 'playboy' (1911 edn., p. 18) and, affectionately by his wife, as 'the biggest rascal in the whole of Ireland'. In *The Mineral Workers* Boyle uses 'playboy' in conjunction with 'devil's darlin' to describe a man 'Hail fellow with every blackguard in the country'. (1910 edn., p. 13).

gap between a gallous story and a dirty deed' (II, 544–7). The speech is climactic, for it explains Pegeen's change of heart over Christy, and leads directly to the burning with the sod. At this point society purges itself of a romantic rebel. If Christy had hitherto expressed the sub-conscious urges of all of us, a point made as early as Patrick Kenny's review in the *Irish Times*,[30] then conventional morality now seizes upon Christy as a scapegoat for the sins of Ireland, or of Adam. Merely to express such a view in direct juxtaposition with the text reveals, however, that Synge is presenting a parody of a serious action, for the blow with the loy is merely a dirty back-yard deed, and the whole thing, Pegeen says, has been inflated out of all proportion by strange and marvellous talk. The whole affair is little more than a 'rape of a bucket', a mock-heroic extravaganza, albeit with serious overtones, and now the game is up. Indeed, the highest moments of Christy's earlier elevation often reached little more than grotesque magnificence – so the *Io triumphe!* of the conquering hero becomes: 'It's Christy! by the stars of God! I'd know his way of spitting and he astride the moon' (III, 149–51). As for Christy's eventual achievement of self-integrity, it is difficult to claim that anything major has been reached if the style is examined: 'you've turned me a likely gaffer in the end of all, the way I'll go romancing through a romping lifetime from this hour to the dawning of the judgement day' (III, 614–17). Cyril Cusack observed that at the end Synge flies from reality and universality.[31] The observation gets to the heart of the matter. On his own description Christy is 'romancing', and he is merely a 'gaffer' who goes 'romping'. Synge is quite explicit. As Patrick Kenny claimed, Ireland had produced the hero it deserved. Does he match up even to Jesse James?

If this is true, it is possible that Synge is doing more than subverting the Abbey school. With objective cynicism and satire he is debunking the dreaming, subjective Synge who idealized the ancient pagan world of the Irish peasantry. Granted that Mayo is not Aran, and granting even that there may be some reflection of the shy but violent Synge in Christy himself, nonetheless, it is not possible to admire either the

[30] 30 January 1907.
[31] See n. 17. above.

society of the shebeen, nor, for much of the time, Mahon's looney. Certainly the simplistic Yeatsian view that Synge underwent a quasi-religious conversion on Aran, will not stand up to critical examination. What one finds instead in Synge is a continuous development expressing itself in a number of artistic experiments where differences of form and rhetoric produce varied solutions to creative problems. The language of *The Playboy*, for instance, is no more that of *Deidre* than the language of *The Rape of the Lock* is that of Pope's *Iliad*. The analogy with Byron, suggested earlier, holds good, for *Don Juan* in becoming more objective than *Childe Harold* turns to burlesque and farce elements which were elsewhere taken with deep subjective seriousness, and sets forth in comic action characters who were previously states of mind of a lonely and brooding author. In so doing lyric and emotive elements from previous work are subsumed in the comic structure, and every flight of passion and lyricism is undercut by setting or by anti-climactic drops into low language.

Synge was attempting something of the same Byronic blend of satire and lyricism in *The Playboy*. If the lyricism is passed lightly by in this introduction, it is because its nature and effectiveness can only be judged truly if the central satiric intention of the work is acknowledged. Yeats asked for a poetic drama. It was felt that the language of the Irish peasantry could provide the basis of such a poetry. Douglas Hyde and Lady Gregory had shown a way. Synge goes further yet, but almost as a parody of the Coole Parkers, pitching the language into the wildest flights of extravagance. The vexed question of its authenticity is a red herring. Whoever troubled whether the speech of a Falstaff or a Volpone were authentic? The critical question is, with what degree of aesthetic seriousness should one take this wild poetic prose?

Christy's wooing of Pegeen may test the issue, for here the element of romance is to the fore, and satire at its lowest ebb. The scene, yet, is not unlike that in Byron when Don Juan and Haidée are alone. In Byron, as in Synge, the setting undercuts the romance. Old Mahon, like Lambro, is likely to intrude at any time and restore us to an unpleasant reality. Further, just as in Byron, if one looks closely at the language, its fanciful beauty is always balancing on the edge of absurdity. Merely compare a fragment from the wooing of Pegeen with one of Synge's Anglo-Irish versions of Petrarch:

CHRISTY

It's little you'll think if my love's a poacher's, or an earl's itself, when you'll feel my two hands stretched around you, and I squeezing kisses on your puckered lips, till I'd feel a kind of pity for the Lord God is all ages sitting lonesome in his golden chair.

PEGEEN

That'll be right fun, Christy Mahon, and any girl would walk her heart out before she'd meet a young man was your like for eloquence, or talk, at all.   (III, 245–52)

Is this the nest in which my Phoenix put on her feathers of gold and purple, my Phoenix that did hold me under her wing, and she drawing out sweet words and sighs from me? Oh, root of my sweet misery, where is that beautiful face, where light would be shining out, the face that did keep my heart like a flame burning? She was without a match upon the earth, I hear them say, and now she is happy in the Heavens.

(*The sight of Laura's house reminds him of the great happiness he has lost*)

The old rhetorical decorums hold true. One passage is comic, the other tragic, hence one is in low style, the other in high. The Petrarch is intended to move tears, and the use of language is therefore emotive. The passage in *The Playboy*, despite its sensuality and the romantic link which is being forged between Christy and Pegeen, nonetheless tends to move laughter. The justly admired 'squeezing kisses on your puckered lips' has the exuberance of Jonson creating a language for the amorous Volpone, but it is not the unambiguous language of the heart, for if God 'sitting lonesome' does not for certain return us to the comic world, Pegeen's 'That'll be right fun' undoubtedly does. If this is true for the lyrical climax of the play, there is no need to prove the point elsewhere. There are flashes of poetic fire in *The Playboy*, and there is much verbal inventiveness, but, as with Byron, every time Pegasus seems to take wing, he turns out to be shackled to the earth. Synge's comments on poetry show him looking for a style which would be earthy, or brutal,[32] and the same ideals appear to hold good in the prose of *The Playboy*. To complain with the unenchanted that this prose is verbose, superficial, predictable in its devices, brings one back to its basis in earthy comedy by a different route. Synge was not intending to be taken seriously. Likewise the language of *The Dunciad* is not as fine as that of the *Aeneid*. But then the *Aeneid* is not as funny as *The Dunciad*.

To take the Aristotelian position that *The Playboy* is low because it is comedy, is not to deny the rich complexity of Synge's art, nor to deny that there are serious matters suggested in the drama: the hints of some primeval myth, the concern with that hunger of imagination that preys upon life, the desire to stretch language to its uttermost. But everything is treated with macabre humour and grotesque invention, and there is a good case for claiming that the serious problems of the play are those not of matter but of manner, of decorum and rhetoric: in what tone should an outrageous statement be made? how naturally should an extravagant or horrid act be played? when should the lyrical and romantic elements in the language be allowed to sound, when should they be burlesqued? Intellectually *The Playboy* has a simple theme: all the world loves a rogue provided his roguery does not hurt us, but the enrichment of the theme comes through the extraordinary variety of tone and response which Synge achieves.

The final speech of the play provides a climactic example. The last speech is Pegeen's because Christy's proclamation of himself as romancing, romping gaffer does not properly resolve the action, leaving us with no more than a likely lad. To Pegeen, therefore, falls the task of lamenting the failure of higher ideals. The burning of Christy has already darkened the mood to something as potentially serious as the end of *Volpone* or *Don Giovanni*, and Synge's final *coup* is to conclude with what may well be a keen. 'Quit my sight', Pegeen

[32] 'In these days poetry is usually a flower of evil or good, but it is the timber of poetry that wears most surely, and there is no timber that has not strong roots among the clay and worms. Even if we grant that exalted poetry can be kept successful by itself, the strong things of life are needed in poetry also, to show that what is exalted, or tender, is not made by feeble blood. It may almost be said that before verse can be human again it must learn to be brutal'. Preface to *Poems and Translations* (1909).

cries out at Shawn, and drawing her shawl over her head, she breaks into wild lamentations: 'Oh my grief, I've lost him surely. I've lost the only playboy of the Western World' (III, 624–5). It is a stinging shock following upon the failure of the comedy to end in the traditional happy marriage, yet the speech is thematically central, for here is the lament of the romantic imagination cheated as always by the failure of the world to fulfil its longings. Further, the word 'playboy' here undergoes its final transmutation, beyond the sense of champion of all sports, as earlier used in praise of Christy as if he were a John Curran of this Western World.[33] Now it involves everything Pegeen has ever longed for in a husband: the passionate sexuality, romantic eloquence of tongue, manly daring, and wondrous reputation of an Irish Antony, 'like the stars of God'.

Yet Pegeen's lament has been cued by Shawn's, 'It's a miracle Father Reilly can wed us in the end of all, and we'll have none to trouble us when his vicious bite is healed' (III, 620–2), which is provocative of laughter – especially delivered on one leg. Her imagination is bogus, for Christy never was an Irish Antony, nor can she even call on the heroic name of the Mahons, but only on the lost 'playboy', which word, if changed utterly here, still retains only too justly its basic sense of blackguard, hypocrite, and play-actor. Finally, Pegeen's grief, if it recalls a keen, is as absurd as it is tragic, for she laments not the dead but a likely lad who has just romped gleefully from the stage.

The inextricable blend of tragedy and comedy at this moment stretches the resources of actress and audience to the utmost. It has been suggested that Synge is on the threshold of the black comedy and the theatre of the absurd of the modern world.[34] O'Casey certainly learnt from him, and it is possible Samuel Beckett also. But the theatrical skill Synge displays here has always been one of the fundamental techniques of comedy, witness the attacks of Aristophanes on war,

[33] John Butler Yeats suggests the link with Curran, noting how crowds would rise early for a duel 'to see the fight, to witness the courage of the combatants and enjoy the wit of Curran', continuing 'We Irish are still what we've always been, a people of leisure; like people sitting at a play, we watch the game of life', *Essays Irish and American* (Dublin and London, 1918), p. 53.

[34] See especially J. L. Styan, *The Elements of Drama* (Cambridge, 1960), and *The Dark Comedy* (Cambridge, 1962).

Falstaff's pretended death, or the art of Cervantes. Synge's manuscripts show him thinking of Jonson, Molière, and Rabelais, and if he succeeds in his purpose then, as Yeats, receiving the Nobel Prize, desired for himself, Lady Gregory, and Synge, the Irish Literary Revival is part of the cultural history not of English literature alone, but of Europe.

NOTE ON THE TEXT

In preparing the text I have used the following sources from the Synge MSS in Trinity College Library, Dublin: the complete typescript prepared by Synge for the printer of the Preface to *The Playboy of the Western World* and Acts I, II, and III; the galley proofs of Act I up to page 16 of the first edition and from page 33 to the entry of Michael, page 70 of that edition (corrected by Synge's hand); the page proofs running from pages 1 to 80 of the first edition (in the main uncorrected). I have also used the facsimile of the 'final' typescript draft sold by Synge to John Quinn deposited in the National Library in Dublin.

I have collated with the MSS sources the following printed editions: (i) the first edition issued by Maunsel & Co. at Dublin in February 1907 with Preface by Synge and a portrait of the author by J. B. Yeats; (ii) the second edition, also 1907; (iii) the issue without Preface or portrait as volume X of the Abbey Theatre Series (1907). A limited edition of (i) of 25 copies on hand-made paper is also recorded, and two advance copies of (i) in different binding and omitting the portrait. I have not seen examples of these. There were no further editions of *The Playboy* in Synge's lifetime, but John Quinn issued a limited edition of Act II in New York (1907) for copyright purposes.

I have also used the extensive MS material reprinted by Professor Ann Saddlemyer in her edition of *The Playboy* in the fourth volume of the Oxford *Collected Works* of Synge (1968), and have benefited greatly from her alert critical attention to the cruces of Synge's text.

In the printed texts I have found no substantive variants, although the second edition is not identical with the first. Numerous revisions were made by Synge in page and galley proof, and a number of substantial departures from the printer's typescript went uncorrected. The typescript Synge sold to Quinn differs so frequently from the printer's that its authority can only be considered that of an advanced draft. I have not found it necessary to incorporate readings from any earlier source.

Although the Oxford text corrects several errors in the first edition issued by Maunsel, and every alteration made merits respectful consideration, nonetheless this New Mermaid edition differs frequently from Professor Saddlemyer's text. The Oxford edition contains no clear textual apparatus. Material appears to have been eclectically introduced into the edition from MS sources sometimes cancelling Synge's instructions in galley, or introducing readings from the Quinn typescript against the authority of the correctly set printer's copy. Alternatively, readings originating from the printer are preferred to both the typescripts. For example: a reading 'PHILLY *nods at* JIMMY' struck out by Synge's hand in galley is reintroduced 'from final typescripts'. In a stage direction correctly set by the printer from his copy '*Filling a sack with straw*' the word 'right' is appended 'from draft G', while, on the other hand, the phrase 'a conceited and foolish man' originating in the print shop is preferred to Synge's 'a conceited and a foolish man' which occurs in both the printer's and Quinn's typescript.

In the present edition a less flexible procedure has been followed. Unless Synge has made an obvious typing error, the authority of the final typescript has been preferred when it differs from the galley proof, and revisions in proof are preferred to the typescript. I have used the Quinn typescript to confirm the printer's and clarify doubtful cases, but do not otherwise quote it. Where galleys do not exist and differences between typescript and page proofs or the first edition occur, consistent judgement is less easy. Substantive variants are therefore given in the apparatus even when rejected.

Concerning accidentals: Synge was a bad speller and erratic in punctuation. Most of the punctuation in the printed text originated

* *

from Maunsel's. Apart from a little tidying-up I have accepted what Synge was prepared to accept.

The following abbreviations are used in the apparatus:

Quinn: the typescript sold by Synge to John Quinn
TS: the typescript prepared for the printer by Synge
G: galley proof
P: page proof
Maunsel: the first edition referred to as (i) above
s.d.:   stage direction

FURTHER READING

David H. Greene and Edward M. Stephens, *J. M. Synge* (New York, 1959).

W. B. Yeats, *Autobiographies* (1955).

W. B. Yeats, *Essays and Introductions* (1961).

W. B. Yeats, *Explorations* (1962).

Lady Gregory, *Our Irish Theatre* (1913).

A. E. Malone, *The Irish Drama* (1929).

Una Ellis-Fermor, *The Irish Dramatic Movement* (revised edn., 1954).

Alan Price, *Synge and Anglo-Irish Drama* (1961).

Donna Gerstenberger, *John Millington Synge* (New York, 1964).

Ann Saddlemyer, *J. M. Synge and Modern Comedy* (Dublin, 1968).

Raymond Williams, *Drama from Ibsen to Eliot* (revised edn., 1964).

For guidance into the extensive periodical literature, see the bibliography and surveys cited in the Introduction, n. 21.

PREFACE

In writing THE PLAYBOY OF THE WESTERN WORLD, as in my other plays, I have used one or two words only that I have not heard among the country people of Ireland, or spoken in my own nursery before I could read the newspapers. A certain number of the phrases I employ I have heard also from herds and fisher-   5
men along the coast from Kerry to Mayo, or from beggar-women and ballad-singers nearer Dublin; and I am glad to acknowledge how much I owe to the folk-imagination of these fine people. Anyone who has lived in real intimacy with the Irish peasantry will know that the wildest sayings and ideas in   10
this play are tame indeed, compared with the fancies one may hear in any little hillside cabin in Geesala, or Carraroe, or Dingle Bay. All art is a collaboration; and there is little doubt that in the happy ages of literature, striking and beautiful phrases were as ready to the story-teller's or the play-wright's   15
hand, as the rich cloaks and dresses of his time. It is probable that when the Elizabethan dramatist took his ink-horn and sat down to his work he used many phrases that he had just heard, as he sat at dinner, from his mother or his children. In Ireland, those of us who know the people have the same privilege. When   20
I was writing 'The Shadow of the Glen', some years ago, I got more aid than any learning could have given me from a chink in the floor of the old Wicklow house where I was staying, that let me hear what was being said by the servant girls in the kitchen. This matter, I think, is of importance, for in countries where   25
the imagination of the people, and the language they use, is rich and living, it is possible for a writer to be rich and copious in his

---

12–13 *Geesala . . . Dingle Bay* Geesala is in north-west Mayo, and local to the action of the play, Carraroe in Galway, Dingle Bay in Kerry in Christy's Province of Munster.
21 *some years ago* 1902.

1

words, and at the same time to give the reality, which is the root of all poetry, in a comprehensive and natural form. In the modern literature of towns, however, richness is found only in sonnets, or prose poems, or in one or two elaborate books that are far away from the profound and common interests of life. One has, on one side, Mallarmé and Huysmans producing this literature; and on the other, Ibsen and Zola dealing with the reality of life in joyless and pallid words. On the stage one must have reality, and one must have joy; and that is why the intellectual modern drama has failed, and people have grown sick of the false joy of the musical comedy, that has been given them in place of the rich joy found only in what is superb and wild in reality. In a good play every speech should be as fully flavoured as a nut or apple, and such speeches cannot be written by anyone who works among people who have shut their lips on poetry. In Ireland, for a few years more, we have a popular imagination that is fiery and magnificent, and tender; so that those of us who wish to write start with a chance that is not given to writers in places where the springtime of the local life has been forgotten, and the harvest is a memory only, and the straw has been turned into bricks.

J.M.S.

January 21*st*, 1907

29 *natural* Maunsel (adequate TS)
39 *joy found only in what* Maunsel (joy of what TS)

PERSONS

THE PLAYBOY OF THE WESTERN WORLD was first produced by the National Theatre Society, Ltd., at the Abbey Theatre, on Saturday, 26th January, 1907, under the direction of W. G. Fay.

CHRISTOPHER MAHON	*W. G. Fay*	
OLD MAHON, *his father, a squatter*	*A. Power*	5
MICHAEL JAMES FLAHERTY (*called* 'Michael James'), *a publican*	*Arthur Sinclair*	
MARGARET FLAHERTY (*called* 'Pegeen Mike'), *his daughter*	*Maire O'Neill*	
SHAWN KEOGH, *her second cousin, a young farmer*	*F. J. Fay*	10
PHILLY O'CULLEN ⎱ *small farmers*	*J. A. O'Rourke*	
JIMMY FARRELL ⎰	*J. M. Kerrigan*	
WIDOW QUIN, *a woman of about thirty*	*Sara Allgood*	
SARA TANSEY ⎫	*Brigit O'Dempsey*	
SUSAN BRADY ⎬ *village girls*	*Alice O'Sullivan*	15
HONOR BLAKE ⎪	*Mary Craig*	
[NELLY] ⎭		

Persons The list of persons has been conflated with the cast list from the first edition. Originally the Widow Quin's name was placed between Pegeen and Shawn, thus obscuring the blood relation of the engaged couple, hence the need of a dispensation to enable them to marry. Saddlemyer notes from the copy registered by the Lord Chamberlain's Office, 27 April 1907, that Nelly's speeches were given to Honor Blake in the first production.

5 *squatter* 'Innumerable squatters had settled themselves, unquestioned, in huts on the mountain sides and in the valleys, without any sufficient provision for their maintenance during the year. They sowed their patches of potatoes early in spring ... trusting to their adroitness and good luck in begging, to keep the family alive till the potato crop again came in' (W. Steuart Trench, *Realities of Irish Life*, 1868, Fitzroy edn., 1966, p. 56). Sometimes tenants sublet to squatters (ibid., p. 72). See also Synge, *Works*, II, 316.

3

PEASANTS $\left\{\begin{array}{l} Harry\ Young \\ U.\ Wright \end{array}\right.$

[A BELLMAN]   20

The Action takes place near a village, on a wild coast of Mayo.
The first Act passes on an evening of autumn, the other two
Acts on the following day.

---

21 *Mayo* Synge describes the north-western seaboard of the county as 'a
waste of turf and bog' and an area of 'the greatest poverty' (*Works*, II,
316).

THE PLAYBOY OF THE WESTERN WORLD

Act 1

SCENE: *Country publichouse or shebeen, very rough and untidy.*
There is a sort of counter on the right with shelves, holding many
bottles and jugs, just seen above it. Empty barrels stand near the
counter. At back, a little to left of counter, there is a door into the
open air, then, more to the left, there is a settle with shelves above
it, with more jugs, and a table beneath a window. At the left there
is a large open fire-place, with turf fire, and a small door into inner
room. PEGEEN, *a wild-looking but fine girl, of about twenty, is*
writing at table. She is dressed in the usual peasant dress.

PEGEEN (*slowly as she writes*)

Six yards of stuff for to make a yellow gown. A pair of lace
boots with lengthy heels on them and brassy eyes. A hat is
suited for a wedding-day. A fine tooth comb. To be sent with
three barrels of porter in Jimmy Farrell's creel cart on the
evening of the coming Fair to Mister Michael James   5
Flaherty. With the best compliments of this season. Margaret
Flaherty.

SHAWN KEOGH (a *fat and fair young man comes in as she signs,*
looks round awkwardly, when he sees she is alone)
Where's himself?

---

1 s.d. *shebeen* often a shop where excisable liquors are sold without a
licence, but here a low wayside public house.

1 s.d. *usual peasant dress* Synge describes the 'usual dress of the women' on
the Mullet Peninsula as 'a short red petticoat over bare feet and legs, a
faded uncertain bodice and a white or blue rag swathing the head'
(*Works*, II, 316n.).

4 *creel cart* a cart with wicker-framed sides, cf. 'creel basket' and *Works*,
II, 226.

PEGEEN (*without looking at him*)

He's coming. (*She directs letter*) To Mister Sheamus Mulroy, Wine and Spirit Dealer, Castlebar.   10

SHAWN (*uneasily*)

I didn't see him on the road.

PEGEEN

How would you see him (*licks stamp and puts it on letter*) and it dark night this half hour gone by?

SHAWN (*turning towards door again*)

I stood a while outside wondering would I have a right to pass on or to walk in and see you, Pegeen Mike (*comes to*   15 *fire*), and I could hear the cows breathing, and sighing in the stillness of the air, and not a step moving any place from this gate to the bridge.

PEGEEN (*putting letter in envelope*)

It's above at the cross-roads he is meeting Philly Cullen; and a couple more are going along with him to Kate Cassidy's   20 wake.

SHAWN (*looking at her blankly*)

And he's going that length in the dark night?

PEGEEN (*impatiently*)

He is surely, and leaving me lonesome on the scruff of the hill. (*She gets up and puts envelope on dresser, then winds clock*) Isn't it long the nights are now, Shawn Keogh, to be   25 leaving a poor girl with her own self counting the hours to the dawn of day?

SHAWN (*with awkward humour*)

If it is, when we're wedded in a short while you'll have no call to complain, for I've little will to be walking off to wakes or weddings in the darkness of the night.   30

PEGEEN (*with rather scornful good humour*)

You're making mighty certain, Shaneen, that I'll wed you now.

---

21 *wake* a watch beside the dead, accompanied by feasting and drinking.

23 *scruff* cf. *Works*, II, 189: 'one grain of the shot cut the scruff off his nose'.

SHAWN

Aren't we after making a good bargain, the way we're only
waiting these days on Father Reilly's dispensation from the
bishops, or the court of Rome. 35

PEEGEEN (*looking at him teasingly, washing up at dresser*)

It's a wonder, Shaneen, the Holy Father'd be taking notice of
the likes of you; for if I was him I wouldn't bother with this
place where you'll meet none but Red Linahan, has a squint
in his eye, and Patcheen is lame in his heel, or the mad
Mulrannies were driven from California and they lost in their 40
wits. We're a queer lot these times to go troubling the Holy
Father on his sacred seat.

SHAWN (*scandalized*)

If we are, we're as good this place as another, maybe, and as
good these times as we were for ever.

PEGEEN (*with scorn*)

As good, is it? Where now will you meet the like of Daneen 45
Sullivan knocked the eye from a peeler, or Marcus Quin, God
rest him, got six months for maiming ewes, and he a great
warrant to tell stories of holy Ireland till he'd have the old
women shedding down tears about their feet. Where will
you find the like of them, I'm saying? 50

SHAWN (*timidly*)

If you don't, it's a good job, maybe; for (*with peculiar emphasis on the words*) Father Reilly has small conceit to have
that kind walking around and talking to the girls.

PEGEEN (*impatiently, throwing water from basin out of the door*)

Stop tormenting me with Father Reilly (*imitating his voice*)

---

34 *dispensation* Saddlemyer quotes Shawn from a rejected draft: 'If he
didn't send his dispensation what way at all would we live a decent life
and we all second cousins for five miles around'.

36 *Shaneen* 'little' Shawn. The suffix 'een' is a diminutive.

46 *peeler* policeman, from Sir Robert Peel, founder of the Irish con-
stabulary.

48 *warrant* certainty.

when I'm asking only what way I'll pass these twelve hours of   55
dark, and not take my death with the fear.

Looking out of door

SHAWN (*timidly*)

Would I fetch you the Widow Quin, maybe?

PEGEEN

Is it the like of that murderer? You'll not, surely.

SHAWN (*going to her, soothingly*)

Then I'm thinking himself will stop along with you when he
sees you taking on, for it'll be a long night-time with great   60
darkness, and I'm after feeling a kind of fellow above in the
furzy ditch, groaning wicked like a maddening dog, the way
it's good cause you have, maybe, to be fearing now.

PEGEEN (*turning on him sharply*)

What's that? Is it a man you seen?

SHAWN (*retreating*)

I couldn't see him at all; but I heard him groaning out, and   65
breaking his heart. It should have been a young man from
his words speaking.

PEGEEN (*going after him*)

And you never went near to see was he hurted or what ailed
him at all?

SHAWN

I did not, Pegeen Mike. It was a dark lonesome place to be   70
hearing the like of him.

PEGEEN

Well, you're a daring fellow, and if they find his corpse
stretched above in the dews of dawn, what'll you say then to
the peelers, or the Justice of the Peace?

SHAWN (*thunderstruck*)

I wasn't thinking of that. For the love of God, Pegeen Mike,   75
don't let on I was speaking of him. Don't tell your father and
the men is coming above; for if they heard that story, they'd
have great blabbing this night at the wake.

PEGEEN

I'll maybe tell them, and I'll maybe not.

SHAWN

They are coming at the door. Will you whisht, I'm saying.   80

PEGEEN

Whisht yourself.

> *She goes behind counter.* MICHAEL JAMES, *fat jovial publican, comes in followed by* PHILLY CULLEN, *who is thin and mistrusting, and* JIMMY FARRELL, *who is fat and amorous, about forty-five*

MEN (*together*)

God bless you. The blessing of God on this place.

PEGEEN

God bless you kindly.

MICHAEL (*to men who go to the counter*)

Sit down now, and take your rest. (*Crosses to* SHAWN *at the fire*) And how is it you are, Shawn Keogh? Are you coming   85
over the sands to Kate Cassidy's wake?

SHAWN

I am not, Michael James. I'm going home the short cut to my bed.

PEGEEN (*speaking across from counter*)

He's right too, and have you no shame, Michael James, to be quitting off for the whole night, and leaving myself lonesome   90
in the shop?

MICHAEL (*good-humouredly*)

Isn't it the same whether I go for the whole night or a part only; and I'm thinking it's a queer daughter you are if you'd have me crossing backward through the Stooks of the Dead Women, with a drop taken.   95

---

89 s.d. *across from* Quinn, TS (across the G, P, Maunsel)

80 *Will you whisht* be silent.
94–5 *Stooks of the Dead Women* cf. *Works*, II, 264: ' "Do you see that sandy head?" he [Danny-boy] said, pointing out to the east, "that is called the Stooks of the Dead Women; for one time a boat came ashore there with twelve dead women on board her, big ladies with green dresses and gold rings, and fine jewelries, and a dead harper or fiddler along with them" '. Synge has altered the location from west Kerry.

PEGEEN

If I am a queer daughter, it's a queer father'd be leaving me
lonesome these twelve hours of dark, and I piling the turf
with the dogs barking, and the calves mooing, and my own
teeth rattling with the fear.

JIMMY (*flatteringly*)

What is there to hurt you, and you a fine, hardy girl would   100
knock the head of any two men in the place?

PEGEEN (*working herself up*)

Isn't there the harvest boys with their tongues red for drink,
and the ten tinkers is camped in the east glen, and the
thousand militia – bad cess to them! – walking idle through
the land. There's lots surely to hurt me, and I won't stop   105
alone in it, let himself do what he will.

MICHAEL

If you're that afeard, let Shawn Keogh stop along with you.
It's the will of God, I'm thinking, himself should be seeing
to you now.

                                    They all turn on SHAWN

SHAWN (*in horrified confusion*)

I would and welcome, Michael James, but I'm afeard of   110
Father Reilly; and what at all would the Holy Father and the
Cardinals of Rome be saying if they heard I did the like of
that?

MICHAEL (*with contempt*)

God help you! Can't you sit in by the hearth with the light
lit and herself beyond in the room? You'll do that surely,   115
for I've heard tell there's a queer fellow above, going mad
or getting his death, maybe, in the gripe of the ditch,
so she'd be safer this night with a person here.

SHAWN (*with plaintive despair*)

I'm afeard of Father Reilly, I'm saying. Let you not be
tempting me, and we near married itself.   120

---

104 *cess* luck.
117 *gripe of the ditch* in the trench (gripe) under the bank (ditch).

PHILLY (*with cold contempt*)

Lock him in the west room. He'll stay then and have no sin to be telling to the priest.

MICHAEL (*to* SHAWN, *getting between him and the door*)

Go up now.

SHAWN (*at the top of his voice*)

Don't stop me, Michael James. Let me out of the door, I'm saying, for the love of the Almighty God. Let me out   125 (*trying to dodge past him*). Let me out of it, and may God grant you His indulgence in the hour of need.

MICHAEL (*loudly*)

Stop your noising, and sit down by the hearth.

Gives him a push and goes to counter laughing

SHAWN (*turning back, wringing his hands*)

Oh, Father Reilly and the saints of God, where will I hide myself to-day? Oh, St. Joseph and St. Patrick and St. Brigid   130 and St. James, have mercy on me now!

SHAWN *turns round, sees door clear, and makes a rush for it*

MICHAEL (*catching him by the coat-tail*)

You'd be going, is it?

SHAWN (*screaming*)

Leave me go, Michael James, leave me go, you old pagan, leave me go, or I'll get the curse of the priests on you, and of the scarlet-coated Bishops of the courts of Rome.   135

With a sudden movement he pulls himself out of his coat, and disappears out of the door, leaving his coat in MICHAEL'*s hands*

MICHAEL (*turning round, and holding up coat*)

Well, there's the coat of a Christian man. Oh, there's sainted glory this day in the lonesome west; and by the will of God I've got you a decent man, Pegeen, you'll have no call to be spying after if you've a score of young girls, maybe, weeding in your fields.   140

PEGEEN (*taking up the defence of her property*)

What right have you to be making game of a poor fellow for minding the priest, when it's your own the fault is, not paying a penny pot-boy to stand along with me and give me courage in the doing of my work?

She snaps the coat away from him, and goes behind counter with it

MICHAEL (*taken aback*)

Where would I get a pot-boy? Would you have me send the   145
bell-man screaming in the streets of Castlebar?

SHAWN (*opening the door a chink and putting in his head, in a small voice*)

Michael James!

MICHAEL (*imitating him*)

What ails you?

SHAWN

The queer dying fellow's beyond looking over the ditch.
He's come up, I'm thinking, stealing your hens. (*Looks over*   150
his shoulder) God help me, he's following me now (*he runs into room*), and if he's heard what I said, he'll be having my life, and I going home lonesome in the darkness of the night.

For a perceptible moment they watch the door with curiosity. Someone coughs outside. Then CHRISTY MAHON, *a slight young man, comes in very tired and frightened and dirty.*

CHRISTY (*in a small voice*)

God save all here!

MEN

God save you kindly.   155

CHRISTY (*going to counter*)

I'd trouble you for a glass of porter, woman of the house.

             He puts down coin

PEGEEN (*serving him*)

You're one of the tinkers, young fellow, is beyond camped in the glen?

CHRISTY

I am not; but I'm destroyed walking.

156 s.d. *to counter* Quinn, TS (to the counter G, P, Maunsel)

MICHAEL (*patronizingly*)

Let you come up then to the fire. You're looking famished   160
with the cold.

CHRISTY

God reward you. (*He takes up his glass and goes a little way
across to the left, then stops and looks about him*) Is it often the
polis do be coming into this place, master of the house?

MICHAEL

If you'd come in better hours, you'd have seen 'Licensed for   165
the sale of Beer and Spirits, to be consumed on the premises,'
written in white letters above the door, and what would the
polis want spying on me, and not a decent house within four
miles, the way every living Christian is a bona fide, saving
one widow alone.   170

CHRISTY (*with relief*)

It's a safe house, so.

> *He goes over to the fire, sighing and moaning. Then he sits
> down putting his glass beside him and begins gnawing a
> turnip, too miserable to feel the others staring at him with
> curiosity*

MICHAEL (*going after him*)

Is it yourself is fearing the polis? You're wanting, maybe?

CHRISTY

There's many wanting.

MICHAEL

Many surely, with the broken harvest and the ended wars.
(*He picks up some stockings, etc., that are near the fire, and
carries them away furtively*) It should be larceny, I'm   175
thinking?

CHRISTY (*dolefully*)

I had it in my mind it was a different word and a bigger.

---

169 *bona fide* a 'person living at a distance of more than three miles and
    therefore entitled under [the] licensing laws to obtain a drink as a
    traveller' (Bushrui). See *Works*, II, 97.

PEGEEN

There's a queer lad. Were you never slapped in school,
young fellow, that you don't know the name of your deed?

CHRISTY (*bashfully*)

I'm slow at learning, a middling scholar only.   180

MICHAEL

If you're a dunce itself, you'd have a right to know that
larceny's robbing and stealing. Is it for the like of that
you're wanting?

CHRISTY (*with a flash of family pride*)

And I the son of a strong farmer (*with a sudden qualm*), God
rest his soul, could have bought up the whole of your old   185
house a while since, from the butt of his tail-pocket, and not
have missed the weight of it gone.

MICHAEL (*impressed*)

If it's not stealing, it's maybe something big.

CHRISTY (*flattered*)

Aye; it's maybe something big.

JIMMY

He's a wicked-looking young fellow. Maybe he followed   190
after a young woman on a lonesome night.

CHRISTY (*shocked*)

Oh, the saints forbid, mister; I was all times a decent lad.

PHILLY (*turning on* JIMMY)

You're a silly man, Jimmy Farrell. He said his father was a
farmer a while since, and there's himself now in a poor state.
Maybe the land was grabbed from him, and he did what any   195
decent man would do.

MICHAEL (*to* CHRISTY, *mysteriously*)

Was it bailiffs?

CHRISTY

The divil a one.

---

184 *strong* well-to-do.

MICHAEL

Agents?

CHRISTY

The divil a one.   200

MICHAEL

Landlords?

CHRISTY (*peevishly*)

Ah, not at all, I'm saying. You'd see the like of them stories
on any little paper of a Munster town. But I'm not calling to
mind any person, gentle, simple, Judge or jury, did the like
of me.   205

They all draw nearer with delighted curiosity

PHILLY

Well, that lad's a puzzle-the-world.

JIMMY

He'd beat Dan Davies' circus, or the holy missioners making
sermons on the villainy of man. Try him again, Philly.

PHILLY

Did you strike golden guineas out of solder, young fellow, or
shilling coins itself?   210

CHRISTY

I did not mister, not sixpence nor a farthing coin.

JIMMY

Did you marry three wives maybe? I'm told there's a sprink-
ling have done that among the holy Luthers of the preaching
north.

CHRISTY (*shyly*)

I never married with one, let alone with a couple or three.   215

PHILLY

Maybe he went fighting for the Boers, the like of the man

---

199 *Agents* landlords' agents who evicted defaulting tenants. For an account
of an eviction see *Works*, II, 88f.

216 *fighting for the Boers* An Irish Transvaal Committee had sent off a
volunteer force under John MacBride to fight against British troops in
the Boer War, which had ended in 1902. (See E. Norman, *A History of
Modern Ireland*, 1971, 241–2.) Earlier drafts contain references to
MacBride, and also to Colonel Lynch, executed for fighting for the Boers.

beyond, was judged to be hanged, quartered and drawn. Were you off east, young fellow, fighting bloody wars for Kruger and the freedom of the Boers?

CHRISTY

I never left my own parish till Tuesday was a week.   220

PEGEEN (*coming from counter*)

He's done nothing, so. (*To* CHRISTY) If you didn't commit murder or a bad, nasty thing, or false coining, or robbery, or butchery, or the like of them, there isn't anything would be worth your troubling for to run from now. You did nothing at all.   225

CHRISTY (*his feelings hurt*)

That's an unkindly thing to be saying to a poor orphaned traveller, has a prison behind him, and hanging before, and hell's gap gaping below.

PEGEEN (*with a sign to the men to be quiet*)

You're only saying it. You did nothing at all. A soft lad the like of you wouldn't slit the windpipe of a screeching sow.   230

CHRISTY (*offended*)

You're not speaking the truth.

PEGEEN (*in mock rage*)

Not speaking the truth, is it? Would you have me knock the head of you with the butt of the broom?

CHRISTY (*twisting round on her with a sharp cry of horror*)

Don't strike me. I killed my poor father, Tuesday was a week, for doing the like of that.   235

PEGEEN (*with blank amazement*)

Is it killed your father?

CHRISTY (*subsiding*)

With the help of God I did surely, and that the Holy Immaculate Mother may intercede for his soul.

PHILLY (*retreating with* JIMMY)

There's a daring fellow.

223 *anything would* Quinn, TS (anything that would G, P, Maunsel)

JIMMY

Oh, glory be to God! 240

MICHAEL (*with great respect*)

That was a hanging crime, mister honey. You should have had good reason for doing the like of that.

CHRISTY (*in a very reasonable tone*)

He was a dirty man, God forgive him, and he getting old and crusty, the way I couldn't put up with him at all.

PEGEEN

And you shot him dead? 245

CHRISTY (*shaking his head*)

I never used weapons. I've no licence, and I'm a law-fearing man.

MICHAEL

It was with a hilted knife maybe? I'm told, in the big world, it's bloody knives they use.

CHRISTY (*loudly, scandalized*)

Do you take me for a slaughter-boy? 250

PEGEEN

You never hanged him, the way Jimmy Farrell hanged his dog from the licence, and had it screeching and wriggling three hours at the butt of a string, and himself swearing it was a dead dog, and the peelers swearing it had life?

CHRISTY

I did not then. I just riz the loy and let fall the edge of it on 255 the ridge of his skull, and he went down at my feet like an empty sack, and never let a grunt or groan from him at all.

---

249 *bloody knives* presumably a reference to the Phoenix Park murders of 1882 in which the Chief Secretary for Ireland, Lord Frederick Cavendish, and his Under Secretary were killed by nationalists armed with surgical knives.

252 *from the licence* to avoid paying the dog licence. Synge tells the story of a 'little man' who knew nothing of dog licences and was lured into the police barracks for a cup of tea. 'He went in cheerfully, and then they put him and his little dog into the lock-up till someone paid a shilling for him and got him out' (*Works*, II, 276).

255 *loy* a long narrow spade.

MICHAEL (*making a sign to* PEGEEN *to fill* CHRISTY's *glass*)

And what way weren't you hanged, mister? Did you bury him then?

CHRISTY (*considering*)

Aye. I buried him then. Wasn't I digging spuds in the 260 field?

MICHAEL

And the peelers never followed after you the eleven days that you're out?

CHRISTY (*shaking his head*)

Never a one of them, and I walking forward facing hog, dog, or divil on the highway of the road. 265

PHILLY (*nodding wisely*)

It's only with a common week-day kind of murderer them lads would be trusting their carcase, and that man should be a great terror when his temper's roused.

MICHAEL

He should then. (*To* CHRISTY) And where was it, mister honey, that you did the deed? 270

CHRISTY (*looking at him with suspicion*)

Oh, a distant place, master of the house, a windy corner of high distant hills.

PHILLY (*nodding with approval*)

He's a close man, and he's right surely.

PEGEEN

That'd be a lad with the sense of Solomon to have for a pot-boy, Michael James, if it's the truth you're seeking one 275 at all.

PHILLY

The peelers is fearing him, and if you'd that lad in the house there isn't one of them would come smelling around if the dogs itself were lapping poteen from the dung-pit of the yard. 280

---

279 *poteen* illicit whiskey.

JIMMY

Bravery's a treasure in a **lonesome place**, and a lad would kill
his father, I'm thinking, would **face a** foxy divil with a pitch-
pike on the flags of hell.

PEGEEN

It's the truth they're saying, and if I'd that lad in the house, I
wouldn't be fearing the loosed khaki cut-throats, or the   285
walking dead.

CHRISTY (*swelling with surprise and triumph*)

Well, glory be to God!

MICHAEL (*with deference*)

Would you think well to stop here and be pot-boy, mister
honey, if we gave you good wages, and didn't destroy you
with the weight of work?   290

SHAWN (*coming forward uneasily*)

That'd be a queer kind to bring into a decent quiet household
with the like of Pegeen Mike.

PEGEEN (*very sharply*)

Will you whisht? Who's speaking to you?

SHAWN (*retreating*)

A bloody-handed murderer the like of . . .

PEGEEN (*snapping at him*)

Whisht I'm saying; we'll take no fooling from your like at all.   295
(*To* CHRISTY *with a honeyed voice*) And you, young fellow,
you'd have a right to stop, I'm thinking, for we'd do our all
and utmost to content your needs.

CHRISTY (*overcome with wonder*)

And I'd be safe this place from the searching law?

MICHAEL

You would, surely. If they're not fearing you, itself, the   300
peelers in this place is decent droughty poor fellows, wouldn't
touch a cur dog and not give warning in the dead of night.

295 *I'm saying* Quinn, TS (I am saying G, P, Maunsel)

---

285 *khaki cut-throats* khaki was first extensively worn by British troops in
the Boer War.
301 *droughty* thirsty.

PEGEEN (*very kindly and persuasively*)

Let you stop a short while anyhow. Aren't you destroyed walking with your feet in bleeding blisters, and your whole skin needing washing like a Wicklow sheep.   305

CHRISTY (*looking round with satisfaction*)

It's a nice room, and if it's not humbugging me you are, I'm thinking that I'll surely stay.

JIMMY (*jumps up*)

Now, by the grace of God, herself will be safe this night, with a man killed his father holding danger from the door, and let you come on, Michael James, or they'll have the best   310 stuff drunk at the wake.

MICHAEL (*going to the door with men*)

And begging your pardon, mister, what name will we call you, for we'd like to know?

CHRISTY

Christopher Mahon.

MICHAEL

Well, God bless you, Christy, and a good rest till we meet   315 again when the sun'll be rising to the noon of day.

CHRISTY

God bless you all.

MEN

God bless you.

> *They go out except* SHAWN, *who lingers at door*

SHAWN (*to* PEGEEN)

Are you wanting me to stop along with you and keep you from harm?   320

PEGEEN (*gruffly*)

Didn't you say you were fearing Father Reilly?

SHAWN

There'd be no harm staying now, I'm thinking, and himself in it too.

322 *no harm* P, Maunsel (no fear TS)

PEGEEN

You wouldn't stay when there was need for you, and let you
step off nimble this time when there's none.   325

SHAWN

Didn't I say it was Father Reilly . . .

PEGEEN

Go on, then, to Father Reilly (*in a jeering tone*), and let him
put you in the holy brotherhoods, and leave that lad to me.

SHAWN

If I meet the Widow Quin . . .

PEGEEN

Go on, I'm saying, and don't be waking this place with   330
your noise. (*She hustles him out and bolts door*) That lad
would wear the spirits from the saints of peace. (*Bustles about,
and then takes off her apron and pins it up in the window as a
blind.* CHRISTY *watching her timidly. Then she comes to him and
speaks with bland good-humour*) Let you stretch out now by 335
the fire, young fellow. You should be destroyed travelling.

CHRISTY (*shyly again, drawing off his boots*)

I'm tired surely, walking wild eleven days, and waking fearful
in the night.

   *He holds up one of his feet, feeling his blisters, and looking at
   them with compassion*

PEGEEN (*standing beside him, watching him with delight*)

You should have had great people in your family, I'm thinking, with the little, small feet you have, and you with a kind 340
of a quality name, the like of what you'd find on the great
powers and potentates of France and Spain.

---

338 s.d. *them* P, Maunsel (it TS)

341 *quality name* Probably the most famous recent Mahon was Charles
James Patrick (1800–91), military adventurer, admiral of the Chilean
fleet, lieutenant in the Tsar's bodyguard, duellist. The reference may be
political as well as heroic, for Mahon moved in the circles of O'Connell
and Parnell. In earlier times the Mahons had been famous chieftains.
342 *potentates of France and Spain* Perhaps she recalls Mahone Bay (Nova
Scotia) and Port Mahon (Minorca), or the continental origins of the Irish
Celts.

CHRISTY (*with pride*)

We were great surely, with wide and windy acres of rich Munster land.

PEGEEN

Wasn't I telling you, and you a fine, handsome young fellow   345
with a noble brow.

CHRISTY (*with a flash of delighted surprise*)

Is it me?

PEGEEN

Aye. Did you never hear that from the young girls where you come from in the west or south?

CHRISTY (*with venom*)

I did not then. Oh, they're bloody liars in the naked parish   350
where I grew a man.

PEGEEN

If they are itself, you've heard it these days, I'm thinking, and you walking the world telling out your story to young girls or old.

CHRISTY

I've told my story no place till this night, Pegeen Mike, and   355
it's foolish I was here, maybe, to be talking free, but you're decent people, I'm thinking and yourself a kindly woman, the way I wasn't fearing you at all.

PEGEEN (*filling a sack with straw*)

You've said the like of that, maybe, in every cot and cabin where you've met a young girl on your way.   360

CHRISTY (*going over to her, gradually raising his voice*)

I've said it nowhere till this night, I'm telling you, for I've seen none the like of you the eleven long days I am walking the world, looking over a low ditch or a high ditch on my north or south, into stony scattered fields, or scribes of bog,

---

364 *scribes* strips of bog from which turf was cut.

where you'd see young, limber girls, and fine prancing   365
women making laughter with the men.

PEGEEN

If you weren't destroyed travelling, you'd have as much talk
and streeleen, I'm thinking, as Owen Roe O'Sullivan or the
poets of the Dingle Bay, and I've heard all times it's the
poets are your like, fine fiery fellows with great rages when   370
their temper's roused.

CHRISTY (*drawing a little nearer to her*)

You've a power of rings, God bless you, and would there be
any offence if I was asking are you single now?

PEGEEN

What would I want wedding so young?

CHRISTY (*with relief*)

We're alike, so.   375

PEGEEN (*she puts sack on settle and beats it up*)

I never killed my father. I'd be afeard to do that, except
I was the like of yourself with blind rages tearing me within,

---

365 *limber* supple.

368 *streeleen* meandering speech.

368 *Owen Roe O'Sullivan* The Gaelic League published his collected songs
'for the first time' in an edition dated 1907 (Irish Texts no. 2). According
to this edition he was born *c.* 1748 at Meentogues 'seven miles to the
east of Killarney', in a district 'permeated with the spirit of learning and
the spirit of song', and died in 1784. 'Though a peasant, and living
among peasants, he writes in the lofty strain and glowing colouring that
bespoke the descendant of the Milesian princes' (xxvi). 'The characteristic
vehemence of the Irish Celt—his enthusiasm, his warmth of nature, his
tenderness of heart—have in his songs found their highest expression'
(xxxvii). Padraic Colum in *The Road Round Ireland* (New York, 1926)
calls him 'the poet of the people ... schoolmaster, potato-digger,
British sailor and soldier, vagrant'. He wrote a poem, part of which
Colum translates, upon a spade. Douglas Hyde in *A Literary History of
Ireland* notes 'his passion for the frail sex was the undoing of him' (1910
edn., p. 604).

369 *the poets of the Dingle Bay* Synge contemplated the idea of making
Christy a ballad-singer from the south and west.

for I'm thinking you should have had great tussling when
the end was come.

CHRISTY (*expanding with delight at the first confidential talk he
has ever had with a woman*)

We had not then. It was a hard woman was come over the   380
hill, and if he was always a crusty kind when he'd a hard
woman setting him on, not the divil himself or his four
fathers could put up with him at all.

PEGEEN (*with curiosity*)

And isn't it a great wonder that one wasn't fearing you?

CHRISTY (*very confidentially*)

Up to the day I killed my father, there wasn't a person in   385
Ireland knew the kind I was, and I there drinking, waking,
eating, sleeping, a quiet, simple poor fellow with no man
giving me heed.

PEGEEN (*getting a quilt out of cupboard and putting it on the sack*)

It was the girls were giving you heed maybe, and I'm
thinking it's most conceit you'd have to be gaming with their   390
like.

CHRISTY (*shaking his head, with simplicity*)

Not the girls itself, and I won't tell you a lie. There wasn't
anyone heeding me in that place saving only the dumb
beasts of the field.

He sits down at fire

PEGEEN (*with disappointment*)

And I thinking you should have been living the like of a king   395
of Norway or the Eastern World.

*She comes and sits beside him after placing bread and mug
of milk on the table*

CHRISTY (*laughing piteously*)

The like of a king, is it? And I after toiling, moiling,
digging, dodging from the dawn till dusk with never a sight
of joy or sport saving only when I'd be abroad in the dark
night poaching rabbits on hills, for I was a divil to poach,   400
God forgive me, (*very naively*) and I near got six months for
going with a dung fork and stabbing a fish.

PEGEEN

And it's that you'd call sport, is it, to be abroad in the darkness with yourself alone?

CHRISTY

I did, God help me, and there I'd be as happy as the sun-   405
shine of St. Martin's Day, watching the light passing the
north or the patches of fog, till I'd hear a rabbit starting to
screech and I'd go running in the furze. Then when I'd my
full share I'd come walking down where you'd see the ducks
and geese stretched sleeping on the highway of the road, and   410
before I'd pass the dunghill, I'd hear himself snoring out, a
loud lonesome snore he'd be making all times, the while he
was sleeping, and he a man'd be raging all times, the while he
was waking, like a gaudy officer you'd hear cursing and
damning and swearing oaths.   415

PEGEEN

Providence and Mercy, spare us all!

CHRISTY

It's that you'd say surely if you seen him and he after drinking for weeks, rising up in the red dawn, or before it maybe,
and going out into the yard as naked as an ash tree in the
moon of May, and shying clods against the visage of the   420
stars till he'd put the fear of death into the banbhs and the
screeching sows.

PEGEEN

I'd be well-nigh afeard of that lad myself, I'm thinking.
And there was no one in it but the two of you alone?

CHRISTY

The divil a one, though he'd sons and daughters walking all   425
great states and territories of the world, and not a one of
them, to this day, but would say their seven curses on him,
and they rousing up to let a cough or sneeze, maybe, in the
deadness of the night.

---

406 *St. Martin's Day* 11 November.
421 *banbhs* piglets (pronounced 'bonnivs').

PEGEEN (*nodding her head*)

Well, you should have been a queer lot. I never cursed my   430
father the like of that, though I'm twenty and more years of
age.

CHRISTY

Then you'd have cursed mine, I'm telling you, and he a man
never gave peace to any, saving when he'd get two months or
three, or be locked in the asylums for battering peelers or   435
assaulting men, (*with depression*) the way it was a bitter life
he led me till I did up a Tuesday and halve his skull.

PEGEEN (*putting her hand on his shoulder*)

Well, you'll have peace in this place, Christy Mahon, and
none to trouble you, and it's near time a fine lad like you
should have your good share of the earth.   440

CHRISTY

It's time surely, and I a seemly fellow with great strength
in me and bravery of . . .

Some one knocks

CHRISTY (*clinging to* PEGEEN)

Oh, glory! it's late for knocking, and this last while I'm in
terror of the peelers, and the walking dead.

Knocking again

PEGEEN

Who's there?   445

VOICE (*outside*)

Me.

PEGEEN

Who's me?

VOICE

The Widow Quin.

PEGEEN (*jumping up and giving him the bread and milk*)

Go on now with your supper, and let on to be sleepy, for if
she found you were such a warrant to talk, she'd be stringing   450
gabble till the dawn of day.

He takes bread and sits shyly with his back to the door

---

439 *lad like* P, Maunsel (lad the like of TS)

PEGEEN (*opening door, with temper*)

What ails you, or what is it you're wanting at this hour of the night?

WIDOW QUIN (*coming in a step and peering at* CHRISTY)

I'm after meeting Shawn Keogh and Father Reilly below, who told me of your curiosity man, and they fearing by this 455 time he was maybe roaring, romping on your hands with drink.

PEGEEN (*pointing to* CHRISTY)

Look now is he roaring, and he stretched out drowsy with his supper and his mug of milk? Walk down and tell that to Father Reilly and to Shaneen Keogh. 460

WIDOW QUIN (*coming forward*)

I'll not see them again, for I've their word to lead that lad forward for to lodge with me.

PEGEEN (*in blank amazement*)

This night, is it?

WIDOW QUIN (*going over*)

This night. 'It isn't fitting,' says the priesteen, 'to have his likeness lodging with an orphaned girl.' (*To* CHRISTY) God 465 save you, mister!

CHRISTY (*shyly*)

God save you kindly.

WIDOW QUIN (*looking at him with half-amused curiosity*)

Well, aren't you a little smiling fellow? It should have been great and bitter torments did rouse your spirits to a deed of blood. 470

CHRISTY (*doubtfully*)

It should, maybe.

WIDOW QUIN

It's more than 'maybe' I'm saying, and it'd soften my heart to see you sitting so simple with your cup and cake, and you fitter to be saying your catechism than slaying your da.

PEGEEN (*at counter, washing glasses*)

There's talking when any'd see he's fit to be holding his head 475 high with the wonders of the world. Walk on from this, for

I'll not have him tormented and he destroyed travelling since
Tuesday was a week.

WIDOW QUIN (*peaceably*)

We'll be walking surely when his supper's done, and you'll
find we're great company, young fellow, when it's of the like   480
of you and me you'd hear the penny poets singing in an
August Fair.

CHRISTY (*innocently*)

Did you kill your father?

PEGEEN (*contemptuously*)

She did not. She hit himself with a worn pick, and the
rusted poison did corrode his blood the way he never overed   485
it, and died after. That was a sneaky kind of murder did win
small glory with the boys itself.

                                   She crosses to CHRISTY'S *left*

WIDOW QUIN (*with good-humour*)

If it didn't, maybe all knows a widow woman has buried her
children and destroyed her man is a wiser comrade for a
young lad than a girl, the like of you, who'd go helter-   490
skeltering after any man would let you a wink upon the road.

PEGEEN (*breaking out into wild rage*)

And you'll say that, Widow Quin, and you gasping with the
rage you had racing the hill beyond to look on his face.

WIDOW QUIN (*laughing derisively*)

Me, is it? Well, Father Reilly has cuteness to divide you now.
(*She pulls* CHRISTY *up*) There's great temptation in a man did   495
slay his da, and we'd best be going, young fellow; so rise up
and come with me.

PEGEEN (*seizing his arm*)

He'll not stir. He's pot-boy in this place, and I'll not have him
stolen off and kidnabbed while himself's abroad.

WIDOW QUIN

It'd be a crazy pot-boy'd lodge him in the shebeen where he   500
works by day, so you'd have a right to come on, young

---

485 *overed* recovered from.

fellow, till you see my little houseen, a perch off on the rising
hill.

PEGEEN

Wait till morning, Christy Mahon. Wait till you lay eyes on
her leaky thatch is growing more pasture for her buck goat   505
than her square of fields, and she without a tramp itself to
keep in order her place at all.

WIDOW QUIN

When you see me contriving in my little gardens, Christy
Mahon, you'll swear the Lord God formed me to be living
lone, and that there isn't my match in Mayo for thatching,   510
or mowing, or shearing a sheep.

PEGEEN (*with noisy scorn*)

It's true the Lord God formed you to contrive indeed.
Doesn't the world know you reared a black ram at your own
breast, so that the Lord Bishop of Connaught felt the elements of a Christian, and he eating it after in a kidney stew?   515
Doesn't the world know you've been seen shaving the foxy
skipper from France for a threepenny bit and a sop of grass
tobacco would wring the liver from a mountain goat you'd
meet lepping the hills?

WIDOW QUIN (*with amusement*)

Do you hear her now, young fellow? Do you hear the way   520
she'll be rating at your own self when a week is by?

514–15 *elements of a Christian* Synge was told by his acquaintance Philly
   Harris, a story 'about a woman from Cahirciveen who suckled a lamb
   at her own breast, and the doctor to whom she later served it as a meal
   "detected the elements of a Christian" in it'. Greene and Stephens,
   op. cit., p. 139.
517–18 *grass tobacco* 'The French [trawlermen] do have two kinds of tobacco;
   one of them is called hay-tobacco, and if you give them a few eggs, or
   maybe nine little cabbage plants, they'll give you as much of it as would
   fill your hat. Then we get a pound of our own tobacco and mix the
   two of them together, and put them away in a pig's bladder – its that
   way we keep our tobacco – and we have enough with that lot for the
   whole winter' (*Works*, II, 241).

PEGEEN (*to* CHRISTY)

Don't heed her. Tell her to go on into her pigsty and not plague us here.

WIDOW QUIN

I'm going; but he'll come with me.

PEGEEN (*shaking him*)

Are you dumb, young fellow?   525

CHRISTY (*timidly*, *to* WIDOW QUIN)

God increase you; but I'm pot-boy in this place, and it's here I'd liefer stay.

PEGEEN (*triumphantly*)

Now you have heard him, and go on from this.

WIDOW QUIN (*looking round the room*)

It's lonesome this hour crossing the hill, and if he won't come along with me, I'd have a right maybe to stop this   530 night with yourselves. Let me stretch out on the settle, Pegeen Mike; and himself can lie by the hearth.

PEGEEN (*short and fiercely*)

Faith, I won't. Quit off or I will send you now.

WIDOW QUIN (*gathering her shawl up*)

Well, it's a terror to be aged a score. (*To* CHRISTY) God bless you now, young fellow, and let you be wary, or there's   535 right torment will await you here if you go romancing with her like, and she waiting only, as they bade me say, on a sheepskin parchment to be wed with Shawn Keogh of Killakeen.

CHRISTY (*going to* PEGEEN *as she bolts door*)

What's that she's after saying?   540

PEGEEN

Lies and blather, you've no call to mind. Well isn't Shawn Keogh an impudent fellow to send up spying on me. Wait till I lay hands on him. Let him wait, I'm saying.

CHRISTY

And you're not wedding him at all?

---

527 *liefer* rather.

PEGEEN

I wouldn't wed him if a Bishop came walking for to join us   545
here.

CHRISTY

That God in glory may be thanked for that.

PEGEEN

There's your bed now. I've put a quilt upon you I'm after
quilting a while since with my own two hands, and you'd best
stretch out now for your sleep, and may God give you a good   550
rest till I call you in the morning when the cocks will crow.

CHRISTY (*as she goes to inner room*)

May God and Mary and St. Patrick bless you and reward
you, for your kindly talk. (*She shuts the door behind her. He
settles his bed slowly, feeling the quilt with immense satisfaction*) Well it's a clean bed and soft with it, and it's great   555
luck and company I've won me in the end of time – two fine
women fighting for the likes of me – till I'm thinking this
night wasn't I a foolish fellow not to kill my father in the
years gone by.

CURTAIN

Act II

SCENE: *as before. Brilliant morning light.* CHRISTY, *looking bright
and cheerful, is cleaning a girl's boots.*

CHRISTY (*to himself, counting jugs on dresser*)

Half a hundred beyond. Ten there. A score that's above.
Eighty jugs. Six cups and a broken one. Two plates. A
power of glasses. Bottles, a school-master'd be hard set to
count, and enough in them, I'm thinking, to drunken all
the wealth and wisdom of the County Clare. (*He puts down*   5
the boot carefully) There's her boots now, nice and decent

1 s.d. *boots* P, Maunsel (boot TS)
2 *Eighty* Maunsel (Seventy TS, P)

for her evening use, and isn't it grand brushes she has?
(*He puts them down and goes by degrees to the looking-glass*)
Well, this'd be a fine place to be my whole life talking out
with swearing Christians, in place of my old dogs and cat,   10
and I stalking around, smoking my pipe and drinking my fill,
and never a day's work but drawing a cork an odd time, or
wiping a glass, or rinsing out a shiny tumbler for a decent
man. (*He takes the looking-glass from the wall and puts it on
the back of a chair; then sits down in front of it and begins   15
washing his face*) Didn't I know rightly I was handsome,
though it was the divil's own mirror we had beyond, would
twist a squint across an angel's brow, and I'll be growing
fine from this day, the way I'll have a soft lovely skin on me
and won't be the like of the clumsy young fellows do be   20
ploughing all times in the earth and dung. (*He starts*) Is she
coming again? (*He looks out*) Stranger girls. God help me,
where'll I hide myself away and my long neck naked to the
world? (*He looks out*) I'd best go to the room maybe till I'm
dressed again.   25

 He gathers up his coat and the looking-glass, and runs into
 the inner room. The door is pushed open, and SUSAN BRADY
 looks in, and knocks on door

SUSAN

There's nobody in it.

           Knocks again

NELLY (*pushing her in and following her, with* HONOR BLAKE *and*
SARA TANSEY)

It'd be early for them both to be out walking the hill.

SUSAN

I'm thinking Shawn Keogh was making game of us and
there's no such man in it at all.

HONOR (*pointing to straw and quilt*)

Look at that. He's been sleeping there in the night. Well,   30
it'll be a hard case if he's gone off now, the way we'll never
set our eyes on a man killed his father, and we after rising
early and destroying ourselves running fast on the hill.

NELLY

Are you thinking them's his boots?

SARA (*taking them up*)

If they are, there should be his father's track on them. Did 35
you never read in the papers the way murdered men do
bleed and drip?

SUSAN

Is that blood there, Sara Tansey?

SARA (*smelling it*)

That's bog water, I'm thinking, but it's his own they are
surely, for I never seen the like of them for whitey mud, 40
and red mud, and turf on them, and the fine sands of the
sea. That man's been walking, I'm telling you.

She goes down right, putting on one of his boots

SUSAN (*going to window*)

Maybe he's stolen off to Belmullet with the boots of Michael
James, and you'd have a right so to follow after him, Sara
Tansey, and you the one yoked the ass cart and drove ten 45
miles to set your eyes on the man bit the yellow lady's nostril
on the northern shore.

She looks out

SARA (*running to window, with one boot on*)

Don't be talking, and we fooled today. (*Putting on other boot*)
There's a pair do fit me well, and I'll be keeping them for
walking to the priest, when you'd be ashamed this place, 50
going up winter and summer with nothing worth while to
confess at all.

HONOR (*who has been listening at door*)

Whisht! there's someone inside the room. (*She pushes door
a chink open*) It's a man.

SARA *kicks off boots and puts them where they were. They
all stand in a line looking through chink*

SARA

I'll call him. Mister! Mister! (*He puts in his head*) Is Pegeen 55
within?

CHRISTY (*coming in as meek as a mouse, with the looking-glass held behind his back*)

She's above on the cnuceen, seeking the nanny goats, the way she'd have a sup of goat's milk for to colour my tea.

SARA

And asking your pardon, is it you's the man killed his father? 60

CHRISTY (*sidling toward the nail where the glass was hanging*)

I am, God help me!

SARA (*taking eggs she has brought*)

Then my thousand welcomes to you, and I've run up with a brace of duck's eggs for your food today. Pegeen's ducks is no use, but these are the real rich sort. Hold out your hand and you'll see it's no lie I'm telling you. 65

CHRISTY (*coming forward shyly, and holding out his left hand*)

They're a great and weighty size.

SUSAN

And I run up with a pat of butter, for it'd be a poor thing to have you eating your spuds dry, and you after running a great way since you did destroy your da.

CHRISTY

Thank you kindly. 70

HONOR

And I brought you a little cut of a cake, for you should have a thin stomach on you, and you that length walking the world.

NELLY

And I brought you a little laying pullet – boiled and all she is – was crushed at the fall of night by the curate's car. Feel 75 the fat of that breast, mister.

---

62 s.d. *taking eggs she has brought* Maunsel (picking package from table TS, P)

---

57 *cnuceen* little hill (pronounced 'knockeen').

CHRISTY

It's bursting, surely.

He feels it with the back of his hand, in which he holds the presents

SARA

Will you pinch it? Is your right hand too sacred for to use at all? (*She slips round behind him*) It's a glass he has. Well, I never seen to this day a man with a looking-glass held to his   80
back. Them that kills their fathers is a vain lot surely.

Girls giggle

CHRISTY (*smiling innocently and piling presents on glass*)

I'm very thankful to you all today . . .

WIDOW QUIN (*coming in quickly, at door*)

Sara Tansey, Susan Brady, Honor Blake! What in glory has you here at this hour of day?

GIRLS (*giggling*)

That's the man killed his father.   85

WIDOW QUIN (*coming to them*)

I know well it's the man; and I'm after putting him down in the sports below for racing, lepping, pitching, and the Lord knows what.

SARA (*exuberantly*)

That's right, Widow Quin. I'll bet my dowry that he'll lick the world.   90

WIDOW QUIN

If you will, you'd have a right to have him fresh and nourished in place of nursing a feast. (*Taking presents*) Are you fasting or fed, young fellow?

CHRISTY

Fasting, if you please.

WIDOW QUIN (*loudly*)

Well, you're the lot. Stir up now and give him his breakfast.   95
(*To* CHRISTY) Come here to me (*she puts him on bench beside her while the girls make tea and get his breakfast*) and let you tell us your story before Pegeen will come, in place of grinning your ears off like the moon of May.

CHRISTY (*beginning to be pleased*)

It's a long story; you'd be destroyed listening.   100

WIDOW QUIN

Don't be letting on to be shy, a fine, gamey, treacherous
lad the like of you. Was it in your house beyond you
cracked his skull?

CHRISTY (*shy but flattered*)

It was not. We were digging spuds in his cold, sloping, stony,
divil's patch of a field.   105

WIDOW QUIN

And you went asking money of him, or making talk of
getting a wife would drive him from his farm?

CHRISTY

I did not, then; but there I was, digging and digging, and
'You squinting idiot,' says he, 'let you walk down now and
tell the priest you'll wed the Widow Casey in a score of days.'   110

WIDOW QUIN

And what kind was she?

CHRISTY (*with horror*)

A walking terror from beyond the hills, and she two score and
five years, and two hundredweights and five pounds in the
weighing scales, with a limping leg on her, and a blinded eye,
and she a woman of noted misbehaviour with the old and   115
young.

GIRLS (*clustering round him, serving him*)

Glory be.

WIDOW QUIN

And what did he want driving you to wed with her?

She takes a bit of the chicken

CHRISTY (*eating with growing satisfaction*)

He was letting on I was wanting a protector from the harsh-

---

116 *young*. G, P, Maunsel (young. (*He* TS). Synge had begun to type
from Quinn a stage direction 'He begins gnawing a chicken leg',
but did not continue. Maunsel queried the TS and Synge
accepted G as set.

ness of the world, and he without a thought the whole while   120
but how he'd have her hut to live in and her gold to drink.

WIDOW QUIN

There's maybe worse than a dry hearth and a widow woman
and your glass at night. So you hit him then?

CHRISTY (*getting almost excited*)

I did not. 'I won't wed her,' says I, 'when all know she did
suckle me for six weeks when I came into the world, and   125
she a hag this day with a tongue on her has the crows and
seabirds scattered, the way they wouldn't cast a shadow on
her garden with the dread of her curse.'

WIDOW QUIN (*teasingly*)

That one should be right company.

SARA (*eagerly*)

Don't mind her. Did you kill him then?   130

CHRISTY

'She's too good for the like of you,' says he, 'and go on now
or I'll flatten you out like a crawling beast has passed under
a dray.' 'You will not if I can help it,' says I. 'Go on,' says
he, 'or I'll have the divil making garters of your limbs
tonight.' 'You will not if I can help it,' says I.   135

He sits up, brandishing his mug

SARA

You were right surely.

CHRISTY (*impressively*)

With that the sun came out between the cloud and the hill,
and it shining green in my face. 'God have mercy on your
soul,' says he, lifting a scythe; 'or on your own,' says I,
raising the loy.   140

SUSAN

That's a grand story.

HONOR

He tells it lovely.

CHRISTY (*flattered and confident, waving bone*)

He gave a drive with the scythe, and I gave a lep to the east.
Then I turned around with my back to the north, and I hit

a blow on the ridge of his skull, laid him stretched out, and   145
he split to the knob of his gullet.

He raises the chicken bone to his Adam's apple

GIRLS (*together*)

Well, you're a marvel! Oh, God bless you! You're the lad
surely!

SUSAN

I'm thinking the Lord God sent him this road to make a
second husband to the Widow Quin, and she with a great   150
yearning to be wedded, though all dread her here. Lift him
on her knee, Sara Tansey.

WIDOW QUIN

Don't tease him.

SARA (*going over to dresser and counter very quickly, and getting
two glasses and porter*)

You're heroes surely, and let you drink a supeen with your
arms linked like the outlandish lovers in the sailor's song.   155
(*She links their arms and gives them the glasses*) There now.
Drink a health to the wonders of the Western World, the
pirates, preachers, poteen-makers, with the jobbing jockies,
parching peelers, and the juries fill their stomachs selling
judgements of the English law.   160

Brandishing the bottle

WIDOW QUIN

That's a right toast, Sara Tansey. Now Christy.

*They drink with their arms linked, he drinking with his left
hand, she with her right. As they are drinking,* PEGEEN MIKE
*comes in with a milk can and stands aghast. They all spring
away from* CHRISTY. *He goes down left.* WIDOW QUIN
remains seated

PEGEEN (*angrily to* SARA)

What is it you're wanting?

---

158 *jobbing jockies* Saddlemyer suggests 'men who travel about breaking in
   horses', but the pejorative link with peelers and juries may indicate
   shifty dealers. In Synge's 'Ballad of a Pauper' those who manipulate
   the law for their own advantage are called 'jobbers'.

SARA (*twisting her apron*)

  An ounce of tobacco.

PEGEEN

  Have you tuppence?

SARA

  I've forgotten my purse.   165

PEGEEN

  Then you'd best be getting it and not be fooling us here.
  (*To the* WIDOW QUIN, *with more elaborate scorn*) And what
  is it you're wanting, Widow Quin?

WIDOW QUIN (*insolently*)

  A penn'orth of starch.

PEGEEN (*breaking out*)

  And you without a white shift or shirt in your whole family   170
  since the drying of the flood. I've no starch for the like of
  you, and let you walk on now to Killamuck.

WIDOW QUIN (*turning to* CHRISTY, *as she goes out with the girls*)

  Well, you're mighty huffy this day, Pegeen Mike, and, you
  young fellow, let you not forget the sports and racing when
  the noon is by.   175

                                              They go out

PEGEEN (*imperiously*)

  Fling out that rubbish and put them cups away. (CHRISTY
  tidies away in great haste) Shove in the bench by the wall.
  (*He does so*) And hang that glass on the nail. What disturbed
  it at all?

CHRISTY (*very meekly*)

  I was making myself decent only, and this a fine country for   180
  young lovely girls.

PEGEEN (*sharply*)

  Whisht your talking of girls.

                                      Goes to counter – right

CHRISTY

  Wouldn't any wish to be decent in a place . . .

---

172 *Killamuck* Father Reilly's 'God-fearing parish' according to a draft.

PEGEEN

Whisht I'm saying.

CHRISTY (*looks at her for a moment with great misgivings, then as a last effort, takes up a loy, and goes towards her, with feigned assurance*)

It was with a loy the like of that I killed my father.   185

PEGEEN (*still sharply*)

You've told me that story six times since the dawn of day.

CHRISTY (*reproachfully*)

It's a queer thing you wouldn't care to be hearing it and them girls after walking four miles to be listening to me now.

PEGEEN (*turning round astonished*)

Four miles?   190

CHRISTY (*apologetically*)

Didn't himself say there were only bona fides living in the place?

PEGEEN

It's bona fides by the road they are, but that lot came over the river lepping the stones. It's not three perches when you go like that, and I was down this morning looking on the   195 papers the post-boy does have in his bag. (*With meaning and emphasis*) For there was great news this day, Christopher Mahon.

She goes into room left

CHRISTY (*suspiciously*)

Is it news of my murder?

PEGEEN (*inside*)

Murder, indeed.   200

CHRISTY (*loudly*)

A murdered da?

PEGEEN (*coming in again and crossing right*)

There was not, but a story filled half a page of the hanging of a man. Ah, that should be a fearful end, young fellow, and it

185 s.d. *at her* Quinn, TS (at her face G, P, Maunsel)

worst of all for a man destroyed his da, for the like of him
would get small mercies, and when it's dead he is, they'd put   205
him in a narrow grave, with cheap sacking wrapping him
round, and pour down quicklime on his head, the way you'd
see a woman pouring any frish-frash from a cup.

CHRISTY (*very miserably*)

Oh, God help me. Are you thinking I'm safe? You were saying at the fall of night, I was shut of jeopardy and I here with   210
yourselves.

PEGEEN (*severely*)

You'll be shut of jeopardy no place if you go talking with a
pack of wild girls the like of them do be walking abroad with
the peelers, talking whispers at the fall of night.

CHRISTY (*with terror*)

And you're thinking they'd tell?   215

PEGEEN (*with mock sympathy*)

Who knows, God help you.

CHRISTY (*loudly*)

What joy would they have to bring hanging to the likes of me?

PEGEEN

It's queer joys they have, and who knows the thing they'd do,
if it'd make the green stones cry itself to think of you swaying
and swiggling at the butt of a rope, and you with a fine, stout   220
neck, God bless you! the way you'd be a half an hour, in great
anguish, getting your death.

CHRISTY (*getting his boots and putting them on*)

If there's that terror of them, it'd be best, maybe, I went on
wandering like Esau, or Cain and Abel, on the sides of Neifin
or the Erris Plain.   225

---

208 *frish-frash* Saddlemyer cites notebook 28: 'Greek sailors eating a sort of
    "frish-frash" Indian meal, raw cabbage, boiled down as thin as gruel'.
224–5 *Neifin . . . Erris Plain* local references. The mountain of Neifin lies
    north-west of Castlebar, and the range in which it is situated stretches
    towards Belmullet in Erris. For an account of the area see *Works*, II,
    325–8.

PEGEEN (*beginning to play with him*)

It would, maybe, for I've heard the Circuit Judges this place is a heartless crew.

CHRISTY (*bitterly*)

It's more than Judges this place is a heartless crew. (*Looking up at her*) And isn't it a poor thing to be starting again, and I a lonesome fellow will be looking out on women 230 and girls the way the needy fallen spirits do be looking on the Lord?

PEGEEN

What call have you to be that lonesome when there's poor girls walking Mayo in their thousands now?

CHRISTY (*grimly*)

It's well you know what call I have. It's well you know it's a 235 lonesome thing to be passing small towns with the lights shining sideways when the night is down, or going in strange places with a dog noising before you and a dog noising behind, or drawing to the cities where you'd hear a voice kissing and talking deep love in every shadow of the ditch, and you 240 passing on with an empty, hungry stomach failing from your heart.

PEGEEN

I'm thinking you're an odd man. Christy Mahon. The oddest walking fellow I ever set my eyes on to this hour today.

CHRISTY

What would any be but odd men and they living lonesome in 245 the world?

PEGEEN

I'm not odd, and I'm my whole life with my father only.

CHRISTY (*with infinite admiration*)

How would a lovely handsome woman the like of you be lonesome when all men should be thronging around to hear the sweetness of your voice, and the little infant children 250 should be pestering your steps I'm thinking, and you walking the roads.

239 *drawing to* Quinn, TS (drawn to G, P, Maunsel)

PEGEEN

I'm hard set to know what way a coaxing fellow the like of
yourself should be lonesome either.

CHRISTY

Coaxing? 255

PEGEEN

Would you have me think a man never talked with the girls
would have the words you've spoken today? It's only letting
on you are to be lonesome, the way you'd get around me now.

CHRISTY

I wish to God I was letting on; but I was lonesome all times,
and born lonesome, I'm thinking, as the moon of dawn. 260

Going to door

PEGEEN (*puzzled by his talk*)

Well, it's a story I'm not understanding at all why you'd be
worse than another, Christy Mahon, and you a fine lad with
the great savagery to destroy your da.

CHRISTY

It's little I'm understanding myself, saving only that my
heart's scalded this day, and I going off stretching out the 265
earth between us, the way I'll not be waking near you another dawn of the year till the two of us do arise to hope or
judgement with the saints of God, and now I'd best be going
with my wattle in my hand, for hanging is a poor thing
(*turning to go*), and it's little welcome only is left me in this 270
house today.

PEGEEN (*sharply*)

Christy! (*He turns round*) Come here to me. (*He goes towards
her*) Lay down that switch and throw some sods on the fire.
You're pot-boy in this place, and I'll not have you mitch off
from us now. 275

260 s.d. *Going to door* Maunsel (omitted TS, G, P)
270 s.d. *turning to go* Maunsel (omitted TS, G, P)

---

274 *mitch off* play truant.

CHRISTY

You were saying I'd be hanged if I stay.

PEGEEN (*quite kindly at last*)

I'm after going down and reading the fearful crimes of Ireland for two weeks or three, and there wasn't a word of your murder. (*Getting up and going over to the counter*) They've likely not found the body. You're safe so with   280 ourselves.

CHRISTY (*astonished, slowly*)

It's making game of me you were (*following her with fearful joy*), and I can stay so, working at your side, and I not lonesome from this mortal day?

PEGEEN

What's to hinder you staying, except the widow woman or   285 the young girls would inveigle you off?

CHRISTY (*with rapture*)

And I'll have your words from this day filling my ears, and that look is come upon you meeting my two eyes, and I watching you loafing around in the warm sun, or rinsing your ankles when the night is come.   290

PEGEEN (*kindly, but a little embarrassed*)

I'm thinking you'll be a loyal young lad to have working around, and if you vexed me a while since with your leaguing with the girls, I wouldn't give a thraneen for a lad hadn't a mighty spirit in him and a gamey heart.

    SHAWN KEOGH *runs in carrying a cleeve on his back, followed by the* WIDOW QUIN

SHAWN (*to* PEGEEN)

I was passing below, and I seen your mountainy sheep eating   295 cabbages in Jimmy's field. Run up or they'll be bursting surely.

---

282 *you were* Maunsel (you are TS, G, P)

---

293 *thraneen* a long slender grass-stalk.
294 s.d. *cleeve* basket.

PEGEEN

Oh, God mend them!

> *She puts a shawl over her head and runs out*

CHRISTY (*looking from one to the other. Still in high spirits*)

I'd best go to her aid maybe. I'm handy with ewes.

WIDOW QUIN (*closing the door*)

She can do that much, and there is Shaneen has long   300
speeches for to tell you now.

> *She sits down with an amused smile*

SHAWN (*taking something from his pocket and offering it to CHRISTY*)

Do you see that, mister?

CHRISTY (*looking at it*)

The half of a ticket to the Western States!

SHAWN (*trembling with anxiety*)

I'll give it to you and my new hat (*pulling it out of hamper*);
and my breeches with the double seat (*pulling it out*); and my   305
new coat is woven from the blackest shearings for three
miles around (*giving him the coat*); I'll give you the whole of
them, and my blessing, and the blessing of Father Reilly
itself, maybe, if you'll quit from this and leave us in the
peace we had till last night at the fall of dark.   310

CHRISTY (*with a new arrogance*)

And for what is it you're wanting to get shut of me?

SHAWN (*looking to the WIDOW for help*)

I'm a poor scholar with middling faculties to coin a lie, so
I'll tell you the truth, Christy Mahon. I'm wedding with
Pegeen beyond, and I don't think well of having a clever
fearless man the like of you dwelling in her house.   315

CHRISTY (*almost pugnaciously*)

And you'd be using bribery for to banish me?

SHAWN (*in an imploring voice*)

Let you not take it badly, mister honey, isn't beyond the
best place for you where you'll have golden chains and shiny

---

303 *Western States* U.S.A.

coats and you riding upon hunters with the ladies of the land.
He makes an eager sign to the WIDOW QUIN *to come to help
him*

WIDOW QUIN (*coming over*)

It's true for him, and you'd best quit off and not have that   320
poor girl setting her mind on you, for there's Shaneen thinks
she wouldn't suit you though all is saying that she'll wed you
now.

CHRISTY beams with delight

SHAWN (*in terrified earnest*)

She wouldn't suit you, and she with the divil's own temper
the way you'd be strangling one another in a score of days.   325
(*He makes the movement of strangling with his hands*) It's the
like of me only that she's fit for, a quiet simple fellow
wouldn't raise a hand upon her if she scratched itself.

WIDOW QUIN (*putting* SHAWN's *hat on* CHRISTY)

Fit them clothes on you anyhow, young fellow, and he'd
maybe loan them to you for the sports. (*Pushing him towards*   330
inner door) Fit them on and you can give your answer when
you have them tried.

CHRISTY (*beaming, delighted with the clothes*)

I will then. I'd like herself to see me in them tweeds and hat.

He goes into room and shuts the door

SHAWN (*in great anxiety*)

He'd like herself to see them. He'll not leave us, Widow
Quin. He's a score of divils in him the way it's well nigh   335
certain he will wed Pegeen.

WIDOW QUIN (*jeeringly*)

It's true all girls are fond of courage and do hate the like of
you.

SHAWN (*walking about in desperation*)

Oh, Widow Quin, what'll I be doing now? I'd inform again
him, but he'd burst from Kilmainham and he'd be sure and   340
certain to destroy me. If I wasn't so God-fearing, I'd near

---

340 *Kilmainham* the notorious Dublin jail, where Parnell was imprisoned.

have courage to come behind him and run a pike into his
side. Oh, it's a hard case to be an orphan and not have your
father that you're used to, and you'd easy kill and make
yourself a hero in the sight of all. (*Coming up to her*) Oh, 345
Widow Quin, will you find me some contrivance when I've
promised you a ewe?

WIDOW QUIN

A ewe's a small thing, but what would you give me if I did
wed him and did save you so?

SHAWN (*with astonishment*)

You? 350

WIDOW QUIN

Aye. Would you give me the red cow you have and the
mountainy ram, and the right of way across your rye path,
and a load of dung at Michaelmas, and turbary upon the
western hill?

SHAWN (*radiant with hope*)

I would surely, and I'd give you the wedding-ring I have, and 355
the loan of a new suit, the way you'd have him decent on
the wedding-day. I'd give you two kids for your dinner, and
a gallon of poteen, and I'd call the piper on the long car to
your wedding from Crossmolina or from Ballina. I'd give
you . . . 360

WIDOW QUIN

That'll do, so, and let you whisht, for he's coming now again.
CHRISTY *comes in very natty in the new clothes.* WIDOW
QUIN *goes to him admiringly*

WIDOW QUIN

If you seen yourself now, I'm thinking you'd be too proud to
speak to us at all, and it'd be a pity surely to have your like
sailing from Mayo to the Western World.

343 *not have* Quinn, TS (not to have G, P, Maunsel)

---

353 *turbary* the right to cut turf or peat for fuel on another's land.
359 *Crossmolina . . . Ballina* The journey from Ballina to Belmullet is some
40 miles of desolate road. Crossmolina is slightly nearer.

CHRISTY (*as proud as a peacock*)

I'm not going. If this is a poor place itself, I'll make myself   365
contented to be lodging here.

WIDOW QUIN *makes a sign to* SHAWN *to leave them*

SHAWN

Well, I'm going measuring the racecourse while the tide is
low, so I'll leave you the garments and my blessing for the
sports today. God bless you!

He wriggles out

WIDOW QUIN (*admiring* CHRISTY)

Well, you're mighty spruce, young fellow. Sit down now   370
while you're quiet till you talk with me.

CHRISTY (*swaggering*)

I'm going abroad on the hillside for to seek Pegeen.

WIDOW QUIN

You'll have time and plenty for to seek Pegeen, and you
heard me saying at the fall of night the two of us should be
great company.   375

CHRISTY

From this out I'll have no want of company when all sorts is
bringing me their food and clothing (*he swaggers to the door,
tightening his belt*), the way they'd set their eyes upon a
gallant orphan cleft his father with one blow to the breeches
belt. (*He opens door, then staggers back*) Saints of glory!   380
Holy angels from the throne of light!

WIDOW QUIN (*going over*)

What ails you?

CHRISTY

It's the walking spirit of my murdered da!

WIDOW QUIN (*looking out*)

Is it that tramper?

CHRISTY (*wildly*)

Where'll I hide my poor body from that ghost of hell?   385

The door is pushed open, and old MAHON *appears on
threshold.* CHRISTY *darts in behind door*

WIDOW QUIN (*in great amusement*)

  God save you, my poor man.

MAHON (*gruffly*)

  Did you see a young lad passing this way in the early morning
  or the fall of night?

WIDOW QUIN

  You're a queer kind to walk in not saluting at all.

MAHON

  Did you see the young lad?   390

WIDOW QUIN (*stiffly*)

  What kind was he?

MAHON

  An ugly young streeler with a murderous gob on him, and a
  little switch in his hand. I met a tramper seen him coming
  this way at the fall of night.

WIDOW QUIN

  There's harvest hundreds do be passing these days for the   395
  Sligo boat. For what is it you're wanting him, my poor man?

MAHON

  I want to destroy him for breaking the head on me with the
  clout of a loy. (*He takes off a big hat, and shows his head in a
  mass of bandages and plaster, with some pride*) It was he did
  that, and amn't I a great wonder to think I've traced him ten 400
  days with that rent in my crown?

WIDOW QUIN (*taking his head in both hands and examining it with
  extreme delight*)

  That was a great blow. And who hit you? A robber maybe?

---

392 *streeler* lazy, untidy person.
395 *harvest hundreds* 'Afterwards we went on to a jetty north of the town,
  where the Sligo boat had just come in. One of the men told us that they
  were taking over a hundred harvestmen to Sligo the next morning,
  where they would take a boat for Glasgow, and that many more would
  be going during the week. This migratory labour has many unsatis-
  factory features; yet in the present state of the country it may tend to
  check the longing for America that comes over those that spend the
  whole year on one miserable farm' (*Works*, II, 320).

MAHON

It was my own son hit me, and he the divil a robber, or
anything else, but a dirty, stuttering lout.

WIDOW QUIN (*letting go his skull and wiping her hands in her
apron*)

You'd best be wary of a mortified scalp, I think they call it,   405
lepping around with that wound in the splendour of the sun.
It was a bad blow surely, and you should have vexed him
fearful to make him strike that gash in his da.

MAHON

Is it me?

WIDOW QUIN (*amusing herself*)

Aye. And isn't it a great shame when the old and hardened do   410
torment the young?

MAHON (*raging*)

Torment him is it? And I after holding out with the patience
of a martyred saint till there's nothing but destruction on,
and I'm driven out in my old age with none to aid me.

WIDOW QUIN (*greatly amused*)

It's a sacred wonder the way that wickedness will spoil a   415
man.

MAHON

My wickedness, is it? Amn't I after saying it is himself has
me destroyed, and he a lier on walls, a talker of folly, a man
you'd see stretched the half of the day in the brown ferns
with his belly to the sun.   420

WIDOW QUIN

Not working at all?

MAHON

The divil a work, or if he did itself, you'd see him raising up
a haystack like the stalk of a rush, or driving our last cow
till he broke her leg at the hip, and when he wasn't at that
he'd be fooling over little birds he had – finches and felts –   425

418 *lier* (ed.) (liar Quinn, TS, G, P, Maunsel)

---

425 *felts* thrushes (the field-fare).

or making mugs at his own self in the bit of a glass we had
hung on the wall.

WIDOW QUIN (*looking at* CHRISTY)

What way was he so foolish? It was running wild after the
girls maybe?

MAHON (*with a shout of derision*)

Running wild, is it? If he seen a red petticoat coming swing-   430
ing over the hill, he'd be off to hide in the sticks, and you'd
see him shooting out his sheep's eyes between the little
twigs and the leaves, and his two ears rising like a hare
looking out through a gap. Girls, indeed!

WIDOW QUIN

It was drink maybe?   435

MAHON

And he a poor fellow would get drunk on the smell of a pint!
He'd a queer rotten stomach, I'm telling you, and when I
gave him three pulls from my pipe a while since, he was
taken with contortions till I had to send him in the ass cart to
the females' nurse.   440

WIDOW QUIN (*clasping her hands*)

Well, I never till this day heard tell of a man the like of that!

MAHON

I'd take a mighty oath you didn't surely, and wasn't he the
laughing joke of every female woman where four baronies
meet, the way the girls would stop their weeding if they seen
him coming the road to let a roar at him, and call him   445
the looney of Mahon's.

WIDOW QUIN

I'd give the world and all to see the like of him. What kind
was he?

MAHON

A small low fellow.

WIDOW QUIN

And dark?   450

---

443 *baronies* divisions of a county.

MAHON

Dark and dirty.

WIDOW QUIN (*considering*)

I'm thinking I seen him.

MAHON (*eagerly*)

An ugly young blackguard.

WIDOW QUIN

A hideous, fearful villain, and the spit of you.

MAHON

What way is he fled?   455

WIDOW QUIN

Gone over the hills to catch a coasting steamer to the north or
south.

MAHON

Could I pull up on him now?

WIDOW QUIN

If you'll cross the sands below where the tide is out,
you'll be in it as soon as himself, for he had to go round ten   460
miles by the top of the bay. (*She points to the door*) Strike
down by the head beyond and then follow on the roadway to
the north and east.

MAHON *goes abruptly*

WIDOW QUIN (*shouting after him*)

Let you give him a good vengeance when you come up with
him, but don't put yourself in the power of the law, for it'd   465
be a poor thing to see a Judge in his black cap reading out
his sentence on a civil warrior the like of you.

She swings the door to and looks at CHRISTY, *who is cowering
in terror, for a moment, then she bursts into a laugh*

WIDOW QUIN

Well, you're the walking playboy of the Western World, and
that's the poor man you had divided to his breeches belt.

CHRISTY (*looking out; then, to her*)

What'll Pegeen say when she hears that story? What'll she be   470
saying to me now?

WIDOW QUIN

She'll knock the head of you, I'm thinking, and drive you
from the door. God help her to be taking you for a wonder,
and you a little schemer making up a story you destroyed
your da. 475

CHRISTY (*turning to the door, nearly speechless with rage, half to
himself*)

To be letting on he was dead, and coming back to his life,
and following after me like an old weasel tracing a rat,
and coming in here laying desolation between my own self
and the fine women of Ireland, and he a kind of carcase
that you'd fling upon the sea . . . 480

WIDOW QUIN (*more soberly*)

There's talking for a man's one only son.

CHRISTY (*breaking out*)

His one son, is it? May I meet him with one tooth and it
aching, and one eye to be seeing seven and seventy divils in
the twists of the road, and one old timber leg on him to
limp into the scalding grave. (*Looking out*) There he is 485
now crossing the strands, and that the Lord God would send
a high wave to wash him from the world.

WIDOW QUIN (*scandalized*)

Have you no shame? (*Putting her hand on his shoulder and
turning him round*) What ails you? Near crying, is it?

CHRISTY (*in despair and grief*)

Amn't I after seeing the love-light of the star of knowledge 490
shining from her brow, and hearing words would put you
thinking on the holy Brigid speaking to the infant saints,

---

490 *star of knowledge* Douglas Hyde in *Love Songs of Connacht* (London and
Dublin, 1893) glosses this Gaelic poetic expression: 'It is making us
understand it is, that there be's double knowledge and greatly increased
sharp-sightedness to him who is in love. The love is like a star, and it
is like a star of knowledge on account of the way in which it opens our
senses, so that we be double more light, more lively and more sharp
than we were before. We understand then the glory and the beauty of
the world in a way we never understood it until that' (p. 41).

and now she'll be turning again, and speaking hard words
to me, like an old woman with a spavindy ass she'd have,
urging on a hill.　　　　　　　　　　　　　　　　　495

WIDOW QUIN

There's poetry talk for a girl you'd see itching and scratching,
and she with a stale stink of poteen on her from selling in the
shop.

CHRISTY (*impatiently*)

It's her like is fitted to be handling merchandise in the
heavens above, and what'll I be doing now, I ask you, and　500
I a kind of wonder was jilted by the heavens when a day was
by.

　　There is a distant noise of girls' voices. WIDOW QUIN *looks*
　　from window and comes to him, hurriedly

WIDOW QUIN

You'll be doing like myself, I'm thinking, when I did destroy
my man, for I'm above many's the day, odd times in great
spirits, abroad in the sunshine, darning a stocking or　505
stitching a shift, and odd times again looking out on the
schooners, hookers, trawlers is sailing the sea, and I thinking
on the gallant hairy fellows are drifting beyond, and myself
long years living alone.

CHRISTY (*interested*)

You're like me, so.　　　　　　　　　　　　　　510

WIDOW QUIN

I am your like, and it's for that I'm taking a fancy to you,
and I with my little houseen above where there'd be myself
to tend you, and none to ask were you a murderer or what at
all.

CHRISTY

And what would I be doing if I left Pegeen?　　　515

WIDOW QUIN

I've nice jobs you could be doing, gathering shells to make

---

494 *spavindy* lame from a tumour of the lower leg.
507 *hookers* in Ireland a one-masted fishing smack.

a white-wash for our hut within, building up a little goose-
house, or stretching a new skin on an old curagh I have, and if
my hut is far from all sides, it's there you'll meet the wisest
old men, I tell you, at the corner of my wheel, and it's   520
there yourself and me will have great times whispering and
hugging . . .

VOICES (*outside, calling far away*)

Christy! Christy Mahon! Christy!

CHRISTY

Is it Pegeen Mike?

WIDOW QUIN

It's the young girls, I'm thinking, coming to bring you to the   525
sports below, and what is it you'll have me to tell them now?

CHRISTY

Aid me for to win Pegeen. It's herself only that I'm seeking
now. (WIDOW QUIN *gets up and goes to window*) Aid me for to
win her, and I'll be asking God to stretch a hand to you in
the hour of death, and lead you short cuts through the   530
Meadows of Ease, and up the floor of heaven to the foot-
stool of the Virgin's Son.

WIDOW QUIN

There's praying!

VOICES (*nearer*)

Christy! Christy Mahon!

CHRISTY (*with agitation*)

They're coming. Will you swear to aid and save me for the   535
love of Christ?

WIDOW QUIN (*looks at him for a moment*)

If I aid you, will you swear to give me a right of way I want,
and a mountainy ram, and a load of dung at Michaelmas, the
time that you'll be master here?

---

518 *curagh* a canoe of lath framework covered by tarred canvas or skin,
aided by a sail but mainly propelled by oars (*Works*, II, 57–8, and illus.,
II, 119). A skin would last eight years (*Works*, II, 281).

CHRISTY

I will, by the elements and stars of night.　　　540

WIDOW QUIN

Then we'll not say a word of the old fellow, the way Pegeen
won't know your story till the end of time.

CHRISTY

And if he chances to return again?

WIDOW QUIN

We'll swear he's a maniac and not your da. I could take an
oath I seen him raving on the sands today.　　　545

GIRLS *run in*

SUSAN

Come on to the sports below. Pegeen says you're to come.

SARA TANSEY

The lepping's beginning, and we've a jockey's suit to fit upon
you for the mule race on the sands below.

HONOR

Come on, will you.

CHRISTY

I will then if Pegeen's beyond.　　　550

SARA

She's in the boreen making game of Shaneen Keogh.

CHRISTY

Then I'll be going to her now.

He runs out followed by the GIRLS

WIDOW QUIN

Well, if the worst comes in the end of all, it'll be great
game to see there's none to pity him but a widow woman,
the like of me, has buried her children and destroyed her　　555
man.

She goes out

CURTAIN

---

551 *boreen* laneway.

Act III

SCENE: *as before. Later in the day.* JIMMY *comes in, slightly drunk.*

JIMMY (*calls*)

Pegeen! (*Crosses to inner door*) Pegeen Mike! (*Comes back again into the room*) Pegeen! (PHILLY *comes in, in the same state*) (*To* PHILLY) Did you see herself?

PHILLY

I did not: but I sent Shawn Keogh with the ass cart for to bear him home. (*Trying cupboards which are locked*) Well, 5 isn't he a nasty man to get into such staggers at a morning wake? and isn't herself the divil's daughter for locking, and she so fussy after that young gaffer, you might take your death with drought and none to heed you?

JIMMY

It's little wonder she'd be fussy, and he after bringing bank- 10 rupt ruin on the roulette man, and the trick-o'-the-loop man, and breaking the nose of the cockshot-man, and winning all in the sports below, racing, lepping, dancing, and the Lord knows what! He's right luck, I'm telling you.

PHILLY

If he has, he'll be rightly hobbled yet, and he not able to say 15 ten words without making a brag of the way he killed his father, and the great blow he hit with the loy.

JIMMY

A man can't hang by his own informing, and his father should be rotten by now.

Old MAHON *passes window slowly*

---

11 *trick-o'-the-loop* a game in which the spectator has to guess the middle loop in a belt.

12 *cockshot-man* 'At one place a man, with his face heavily blackened, except one cheek and eye – an extraordinary effect – was standing shots of a wooden ball behind a board with a large hole in the middle, at three shots a penny. When I came past half an hour afterwards he had been hit in the mouth – by a girl some one told me – but seemed as cheerful as ever' (*Works*, II, 274).

PHILLY

Supposing a man's digging spuds in that field with a long   20
spade, and supposing he flings up the two halves of that
skull, what'll be said then in the papers and the courts of law?

JIMMY

They'd say it was an old Dane, maybe, was drowned in the
flood. (*Old* MAHON *comes in and sits down near door listening*)
Did you never hear tell of the skulls they have in the city of   25
Dublin, ranged out like blue jugs in a cabin of Connaught?

PHILLY

And you believe that?

JIMMY (*pugnaciously*)

Didn't a lad see them and he after coming from harvesting
in the Liverpool boat? 'They have them there,' says he,
'making a show of the great people there was one time   30
walking the world. White skulls and black skulls and yellow
skulls, and some with full teeth, and some haven't only but
one.'

PHILLY

It was no lie, maybe, for when I was a young lad, there was
a graveyard beyond the house with the remnants of a man   35
who had thighs as long as your arm. He was a horrid man,
I'm telling you, and there was many a fine Sunday I'd put
him together for fun, and he with shiny bones, you
wouldn't meet the like of these days in the cities of the world.

MAHON (*getting up*)

You wouldn't is it? Lay your eyes on that skull, and tell me   40
where and when there was another the like of it, is splintered
only from the blow of a loy.

PHILLY

Glory be to God! And who hit you at all?

MAHON (*triumphantly*)

It was my own son hit me. Would you believe that?

JIMMY

Well, there's wonders hidden in the heart of man!   45

PHILLY (*suspiciously*)

    And what way was it done?

MAHON (*wandering about the room*)

    I'm after walking hundreds and long scores of miles, winning clean beds and the fill of my belly four times in the day, and I doing nothing but telling stories of that naked truth. (*He comes to them a little aggressively*) Give me a supeen and   50 I'll tell you now.

      WIDOW QUIN *comes in and stands aghast behind him. He is facing* JIMMY *and* PHILLY, *who are on the left*

JIMMY

    Ask herself beyond. She's the stuff hidden in her shawl.

WIDOW QUIN (*coming to* MAHON *quickly*)

    You here, is it? You didn't go far at all?

MAHON

    I seen the coasting steamer passing, and I got a drought upon me and a cramping leg, so I said, 'The divil go along with   55 him,' and turned again. (*Looking under her shawl*) And let you give me a supeen, for I'm destroyed travelling since Tuesday was a week.

WIDOW QUIN (*getting a glass, in a cajoling tone*)

    Sit down then by the fire and take your ease for a space. You've a right to be destroyed indeed, with your walking, and   60 fighting, and facing the sun. (*Giving him poteen from a stone jar she has brought in*) There now is a drink for you, and may it be to your happiness and length of life.

MAHON (*taking glass greedily, and sitting down by fire*)

    God increase you!

WIDOW QUIN (*taking men to the right stealthily*)

    Do you know what? That man's raving from his wound   65 today, for I met him a while since telling a rambling tale of a tinker had him destroyed. Then he heard of Christy's deed, and he up and says it was his son had cracked his skull. Oh, isn't madness a fright, for he'll go killing someone yet, and he thinking it's the man has struck him so.   70

JIMMY (*entirely convinced*)

It's a fright surely. I knew a party was kicked in the head by
a red mare, and he went killing horses a great while, till he eat
the insides of a clock and died after.

PHILLY (*with suspicion*)

Did he see Christy?

WIDOW QUIN

He didn't. (*With a warning gesture*) Let you not be putting   75
him in mind of him, or you'll be likely summoned if there's
murder done. (*Looking round at* MAHON) Whisht! He's listening. Wait now till you hear me taking him easy and unravelling
all. (*She goes to* MAHON) And what way are you feeling,
mister? Are you in contentment now?   80

MAHON (*slightly emotional from his drink*)

I'm poorly only, for it's a hard story the way I'm left today,
when it was I did tend him from his hour of birth, and he a
dunce never reached his second book, the way he'd come
from school, many's the day, with his legs lamed under him,
and he blackened with his beatings like a tinker's ass. It's a   85
hard story, I'm saying, the way some do have their next and
nighest raising up a hand of murder on them, and some is
lonesome getting their death with lamentation in the dead of
night.

WIDOW QUIN (*not knowing what to say*)

To hear you talking so quiet, who'd know you were the same   90
fellow we seen pass today?

MAHON

I'm the same surely. The wrack and ruin of three score
years; and it's a terror to live that length, I tell you, and to
have your sons going to the dogs against you, and you
wore out scolding them, and skelping them, and God knows   95
what.

---

95 *skelping* smacking, beating.

PHILLY (*to* JIMMY)

He's not raving. (*To* WIDOW QUIN) Will you ask him what kind was his son?

WIDOW QUIN (*to* MAHON *with a peculiar look*)

Was your son that hit you a lad of one year and a score maybe, a great hand at racing and lepping and licking the   100
world?

MAHON (*turning on her with a roar of rage*)

Didn't you hear me say he was the fool of men, the way from this out he'll know the orphan's lot with old and young making game of him and they swearing, raging, kicking at him like a mangy cur.   105

> *A great burst of cheering outside, some way off*

MAHON (*putting his hands to his ears*)

What in the name of God do they want roaring below?

WIDOW QUIN (*with the shade of a smile*)

They're cheering a young lad, the champion playboy of the Western World.

> *More cheering*

MAHON (*going to window*)

It'd split my heart to hear them, and I with pulses in my brain-pan for a week gone by. Is it racing they are?   110

JIMMY (*looking from door*)

It is then. They are mounting him for the mule race will be run upon the sands. That's the playboy on the winkered mule.

MAHON (*puzzled*)

That lad, is it? If you said it was a fool he was, I'd have laid a mighty oath he was the likeness of my wandering son.   115
(*Uneasily, putting his hand to his head*) Faith, I'm thinking I'll go walking for to view the race.

WIDOW QUIN (*stopping him, sharply*)

You will not. You'd best take the road to Belmullet, and

---

112 *winkered* blinkered.

not be dilly-dallying in this place where there isn't a spot you
could sleep.   120

PHILLY (*coming forward*)

Don't mind her. Mount there on the bench and you'll have
a view of the whole. They're hurrying before the tide will
rise, and it'd be near over if you went down the pathway
through the crags below.

MAHON (*mounts on bench*, WIDOW QUIN *beside him*)

That's a right view again the edge of the sea. They're   125
coming now from the point. He's leading. Who is he at all?

WIDOW QUIN

He's the champion of the world, I tell you, and there isn't a
hap'orth isn't falling lucky to his hands today.

PHILLY (*looking out, interested in the race*)

Look at that. They're pressing him now.

JIMMY

He'll win it yet.   130

PHILLY

Take your time, Jimmy Farrell. It's too soon to say.

WIDOW QUIN (*shouting*)

Watch him taking the gate. There's riding.

JIMMY (*cheering*)

More power to the young lad!

MAHON

He's passing the third.

JIMMY

He'll lick them yet!   135

WIDOW QUIN

He'd lick them if he was running races with a score itself.

MAHON

Look at the mule he has, kicking the stars.

WIDOW QUIN

There was a lep! (*Catching hold of* MAHON *in her excitement*)
He's fallen! He's mounted again! Faith, he's passing them
all!   140

131 *your* Quinn, TS (you G, P, Maunsel)

JIMMY

Look at him skelping her!

PHILLY

And the mountain girls hooshing him on!

JIMMY

It's the last turn! The post's cleared for them now!

MAHON

Look at the narrow place. He'll be into the bogs! (*With a yell*) Good rider! He's through it again!   145

JIMMY

He's neck and neck!

MAHON

Good boy to him! Flames, but he's in!

Great cheering, in which all join

MAHON (*with hesitation*)

What's that? They're raising him up. They're coming this way. (*With a roar of rage and astonishment*) It's Christy! by the stars of God! I'd know his way of spitting and he   150 astride the moon.

He jumps down and makes a run for the door, but WIDOW QUIN *catches him and pulls him back*

WIDOW QUIN

Stay quiet, will you. That's not your son. (*To* JIMMY) Stop him, or you'll get a month for the abetting of manslaughter and be fined as well.

JIMMY

I'll hold him.   155

MAHON (*struggling*)

Let me out! Let me out the lot of you! till I have my vengeance on his head today.

---

150 *stars* Maunsel (hairs TS, G, P)

---

143 *The post's cleared* Synge records a country race on the sands: 'the course led out along the edge of the sea to a post some distance away, back again to the starting point, round a post, and out and back once more'. The excited crowd interfered with the race (*Works*, II, 272–4).

WIDOW QUIN (*shaking him, vehemently*)

That's not your son. That's a man is going to make a marriage with the daughter of this house, a place with fine trade,
with a licence, and with poteen too.   160

MAHON (*amazed*)

That man marrying a decent and a moneyed girl! Is it mad
yous are? Is it in a crazy-house for females that I'm landed
now?

WIDOW QUIN

It's mad yourself is with the blow upon your head. That
lad is the wonder of the Western World.   165

MAHON

I seen it's my son.

WIDOW QUIN

You seen that you're mad. (*Cheering outside*) Do you hear
them cheering him in the zig-zags of the road? Aren't you
after saying that your son's a fool, and how would they be
cheering a true idiot born?   170

MAHON (*getting distressed*)

It's maybe out of reason that that man's himself. (*Cheering
again*) There's none surely will go cheering him. Oh, I'm
raving with a madness that would fright the world! (*He sits
down with his hand to his head*) There was one time I seen ten
scarlet divils letting on they'd cork my spirit in a gallon can; 175
and one time I seen rats as big as badgers sucking the life
blood from the butt of my lug; but I never till this day con-
fused that dribbling idiot with a likely man. I'm destroyed
surely.

WIDOW QUIN

And who'd wonder when it's your brain-pan that is gaping 180
now?

MAHON

Then the blight of the sacred drought upon myself and him,

173 *a madness* Maunsel (the madness TS, G, P)

---

177 *butt of my lug* lobe of my ear.

for I never went mad to this day, and I not three weeks with
the Limerick girls drinking myself silly, and parlatic from
the dusk to dawn. (*To* WIDOW QUIN, *suddenly*) Is my visage   185
astray?

WIDOW QUIN

It is then. You're a sniggering maniac, a child could see.

MAHON (*getting up more cheerfully*)

Then I'd best be going to the Union beyond, and there'll be
a welcome before me, I tell you (*with great pride*), and I
a terrible and fearful case, the way that there I was one time,   190
screeching in a straightened waistcoat, with seven doctors
writing out my sayings in a printed book. Would you believe
that?

WIDOW QUIN

If you're a wonder itself, you'd best be hasty, for them
lads caught a maniac one time and pelted the poor creature   195
till he ran out, raving and foaming, and was drowned in the
sea.

MAHON (*with philosophy*)

It's true mankind is the divil when your head's astray.
Let me out now and I'll slip down the boreen, and not see
them so.   200

WIDOW QUIN (*showing him out*)

That's it. Run to the right, and not a one will see.

He runs off

PHILLY (*wisely*)

You're at some gaming, Widow Quin; but I'll walk after him
and give him his dinner and a time to rest, and I'll see
then if he's raving or as sane as you.

WIDOW QUIN (*annoyed*)

If you go near that lad, let you be wary of your head, I'm   205
saying. Didn't you hear him telling he was crazed at times?

---

188 *Union* the workhouse of a Poor Law Union: 'looked on with supreme
horror by the peasants. The madhouse, which they know better, is less
dreaded' (*Works*, II, 217).

PHILLY

I heard him telling a power; and I'm thinking we'll have
right sport, before night will fall.

He goes out

JIMMY

Well, Philly's a conceited and a foolish man. How could
that madman have his senses and his brain-pan slit? I'll   210
go after them and see him turn on Philly now.

He goes. WIDOW QUIN *hides poteen behind counter. Then
hubbub outside*

VOICES

There you are! Good jumper! Grand lepper! Darlint boy!
He's the racer! Bear him on, will you!

CHRISTY *comes in, in jockey's dress, with* PEGEEN MIKE, SARA,
and other girls, and men

PEGEEN (*to crowd*)

Go on now and don't destroy him and he drenching with
sweat. Go along, I'm saying, and have your tug-of-warring   215
till he's dried his skin.

CROWD

Here's his prizes! A bagpipes! A fiddle was played by a poet
in the years gone by! A flat and three-thorned blackthorn
would lick the scholars out of Dublin town!

CHRISTY (*taking prizes from the men*)

Thank you kindly, the lot of you. But you'd say it was little   220
only I did this day if you'd seen me a while since striking my
one single blow.

TOWN CRIER (*outside, ringing a bell*)

Take notice, last event of this day! Tug-of-warring on the
green below! Come on, the lot of you! Great achievements
for all Mayo men!   225

PEGEEN

Go on, and leave him for to rest and dry. Go on, I tell you,

209 *and a foolish* Quinn, TS (and foolish G, P, Maunsel)

218 *blackthorn* a walking stick.

for he'll do no more. (*She hustles crowd out;* WIDOW QUIN *following them*)

MEN (*going*)

Come on then. Good luck for the while!

PEGEEN (*radiantly, wiping his face with her shawl*)

Well, you're the lad, and you'll have great times from this out when you could win that wealth of prizes, and you   230 sweating in the heat of noon!

CHRISTY (*looking at her with delight*)

I'll have great times if I win the crowning prize I'm seeking now, and that's your promise that you'll wed me in a fortnight, when our banns is called.

PEGEEN (*backing away from him*)

You've right daring to go ask me that, when all knows you'll   235 be starting to some girl in your own townland, when your father's rotten in four months, or five.

CHRISTY (*indignantly*)

Starting from you, is it? (*He follows her*) I will not, then, and when the airs is warming in four months, or five, it's then yourself and me should be pacing Neifin in the dews of night,   240 the times sweet smells do be rising, and you'd see a little, shiny new moon, maybe, sinking on the hills.

PEGEEN (*looking at him playfully*)

And it's that kind of a poacher's love you'd make, Christy Mahon, on the sides of Neifin, when the night is down?

CHRISTY

It's little you'll think if my love's a poacher's, or an earl's   245 itself, when you'll feel my two hands stretched around you, and I squeezing kisses on your puckered lips, till I'd feel a kind of pity for the Lord God is all ages sitting lonesome in his golden chair.

---

236 *townland* a division of land of varying extent. 'Two or three cabins gathered together were sufficient to form a town, and the land adjoining thereto is called a townland'. Maria Edgeworth, *Ennui*, ch. 8.

PEGEEN

> That'll be right fun, Christy Mahon, and any girl would walk   250
> her heart out before she'd meet a young man was your like
> for eloquence, or talk, at all.

CHRISTY (*encouraged*)

> Let you wait, to hear me talking, till we're astray in Erris,
> when Good Friday's by, drinking a sup from a well, and
> making mighty kisses with our wetted mouths, or gaming in a   255
> gap of sunshine, with yourself stretched back unto your
> necklace, in the flowers of the earth.

PEGEEN (*in a lower voice, moved by his tone*)

> I'd be nice so, is it?

CHRISTY (*with rapture*)

> If the mitred bishops seen you that time, they'd be the like
> of the holy prophets, I'm thinking, do be straining the bars   260
> of Paradise to lay eyes on the Lady Helen of Troy, and she
> abroad, pacing back and forward, with a nosegay in her
> golden shawl.

PEGEEN (*with real tenderness*)

> And what is it I have, Christy Mahon, to make me fitting
> entertainment for the like of you, that has such poet's   265
> talking, and such bravery of heart?

CHRISTY (*in a low voice*)

> Isn't there the light of seven heavens in your heart alone,
> the way you'll be an angel's lamp to me from this out, and
> I abroad in the darkness, spearing salmons in the Owen, or
> the Carrowmore?   270

PEGEEN

> If I was your wife, I'd be along with you those nights,
> Christy Mahon, the way you'd see I was a great hand at
> coaxing baliffs, or coining funny nick-names for the stars of
> night.

CHRISTY

> You, is it? Taking your death in the hailstones, or the fogs of   275
> dawn.

275 *or the fogs* TS (or the rains Quinn, or in the fogs G, P, Maunsel)

PEGEEN

Yourself and me would shelter easy in a narrow bush, (*with a qualm of dread*) but we're only talking, maybe, for this would be a poor, thatched place to hold a fine lad is the like of you. 280

CHRISTY (*putting his arm round her*)

If I wasn't a good Christian, it's on my naked knees I'd be saying my prayers and paters to every jackstraw you have roofing your head, and every stony pebble is paving the laneway to your door.

PEGEEN (*radiantly*)

If that's the truth, I'll be burning candles from this out to 285 the miracles of God have brought you from the south today, and I, with my gowns bought ready, the way that I can wed you, and not wait at all.

CHRISTY

It's miracles, and that's the truth. Me there toiling a long while, and walking a long while, not knowing at all I was 290 drawing all times nearer to this holy day.

PEGEEN

And myself, a girl, was tempted often to go sailing the seas till I'd marry a Jew-man, with ten kegs of gold, and I not knowing at all there was the like of you drawing nearer, like the stars of God. 295

CHRISTY

And to think I'm long years hearing women talking that talk, to all bloody fools, and this the first time I've heard the like of your voice talking sweetly for my own delight.

PEGEEN

And to think it's me is talking sweetly, Christy Mahon, and I the fright of seven townlands for my biting tongue. Well, 300 the heart's a wonder; and, I'm thinking, there won't be our like in Mayo, for gallant lovers, from this hour, today.

286 *God have* Quinn, TS (God that have G, P, Maunsel)

282 *paters* The Lord's Prayer.

(*Drunken singing is heard outside*) There's my father coming
from the wake, and when he's had his sleep we'll tell him,
for he's peaceful then.   305

They separate

MICHAEL (*singing outside*)

> The jailer and the turnkey
> They quickly ran us down,
> And brought us back as prisoners
> Once more to Cavan town.

He comes in supported by SHAWN

> There we lay bewailing   310
> All in a prison bound . . .

He sees CHRISTY. *Goes and shakes him drunkenly by the hand,*
while PEGEEN *and* SHAWN *talk on the left*

MICHAEL (*to* CHRISTY)

The blessing of God and the holy angels on your head, young
fellow. I hear tell you're after winning all in the sports
below; and wasn't it a shame I didn't bear you along with
me to Kate Cassidy's wake, a fine, stout lad, the like of you, 315
for you'd never see the match of it for flows of drink, the
way when we sunk her bones at noonday to her narrow grave,
there were five men, aye, and six men, stretched out retching
speechless on the holy stones.

CHRISTY (*uneasily, watching* PEGEEN)

Is that the truth?   320

MICHAEL

It is then, and aren't you a louty schemer to go burying your
poor father unbeknownst when you'd a right to throw him
on the crupper of a Kerry mule and drive him westwards,
like holy Joseph in the days gone by, the way we could have
given him a decent burial, and not have him rotting beyond,   325

---

317 *to her* Quinn, TS (in her P, Maunsel)

---

306 *Michael's song* 'John McGoldrick and the Quaker's Daughter'. The
words and music are given below, pp. 86–7.

and not a Christian drinking a smart drop to the glory of his
soul?

CHRISTY (*gruffly*)

It's well enough he's lying, for the likes of him.

MICHAEL (*slapping him on the back*)

Well, aren't you a hardened slayer? It'll be a poor thing for
the household man where you go sniffing for a female wife;   330
and (*pointing to* SHAWN) look beyond at that shy and decent
Christian I have chosen for my daughter's hand, and I after
getting the gilded dispensation this day for to wed them
now.

CHRISTY

And you'll be wedding them this day, is it?   335

MICHAEL (*drawing himself up*)

Aye. Are you thinking, if I'm drunk itself, I'd leave my
daughter living single with a little frisky rascal is the like
of you?

PEGEEN (*breaking away from* SHAWN)

Is it the truth the dispensation's come?

MICHAEL (*triumphantly*)

Father Reilly's after reading it in gallous Latin, and 'It's   340
come in the nick of time,' says he; 'so I'll wed them in a
hurry, dreading that young gaffer who'd capsize the stars.'

PEGEEN (*fiercely*)

He's missed his nick of time, for it's that lad, Christy Mahon,
that I'm wedding now.

MICHAEL (*loudly with horror*)

You'd be making him a son to me, and he wet and crusted   345
with his father's blood?

PEGEEN

Aye. Wouldn't it be a bitter thing for a girl to go marrying
the like of Shaneen, and he a middling kind of scarecrow,
with no savagery or fine words in him at all?

---

340 *gallous* fine, spirited.

MICHAEL (*gasping and sinking on a chair*)

Oh, aren't you a heathen daughter to go shaking the fat of   350
my heart, and I swamped and drownded with the weight of
drink? Would you have them turning on me the way that I'd
be roaring to the dawn of day with the wind upon my heart?
Have you not a word to aid me, Shaneen? Are you not
jealous at all?   355

SHAWN (*in great misery*)

I'd be afeard to be jealous of a man did slay his da.

PEGEEN

Well, it'd be a poor thing to go marrying your like. I'm seeing there's a world of peril for an orphan girl, and isn't it a
great blessing I didn't wed you, before himself came walking from the west or south?   360

SHAWN

It's a queer story you'd go picking a dirty tramp up from the
highways of the world.

PEGEEN (*playfully*)

And you think you're a likely beau to go straying along with,
the shiny Sundays of the opening year, when it's sooner on a
bullock's liver you'd put a poor girl thinking then on the lily   365
or the rose?

SHAWN

And have you no mind of my weight of passion, and the holy
dispensation, and the drift of heifers I am giving, and the
golden ring?

PEGEEN

I'm thinking you're too fine for the like of me, Shawn Keogh   370
of Killakeen, and let you go off till you'd find a radiant lady
with droves of bullocks on the plains of Meath, and herself

359 *great* Maunsel (wondrous TS, P)

---

368 *drift* drove.
372 *Meath* the fertile region of the east.

bedizened in the diamond jewelleries of Pharaoh's ma. That'd
be your match, Shaneen. So God save you now!

She retreats behind CHRISTY

SHAWN

Won't you hear me telling you . . .?   375

CHRISTY (*with ferocity*)

Take yourself from this, young fellow, or I'll maybe add a
murder to my deeds today.

MICHAEL (*springing up with a shriek*)

Murder is it? Is it mad yous are? Would you go making
murder in this place, and it piled with poteen for our drink
tonight? Go on to the foreshore if it's fighting you want,   380
where the rising tide will wash all traces from the memory of
man.

Pushing SHAWN *towards* CHRISTY

SHAWN (*shaking himself free, and getting behind* MICHAEL)

I'll not fight him, Michael James. I'd liefer live a bachelor,
simmering in passions to the end of time, than face a lepping
savage the like of him has descended from the Lord knows   385
where. Strike him yourself, Michael James, or you'll lose
my drift of heifers and my blue bull from Sneem.

MICHAEL

Is it me fight him, when it's father-slaying he's bred to
now? (*Pushing* SHAWN) Go on you fool and fight him now.

SHAWN (*coming forward a little*)

Will I strike him with my hand?   390

MICHAEL

Take the loy is on your western side.

SHAWN

I'd be afeard of the gallows if I struck with that.

CHRISTY (*taking up the loy*)

Then I'll make you face the gallows or quit off from this.

SHAWN *flies out of the door*

391 *loy is* Maunsel (Loy's TS, P)

387 *Sneem* in Kerry, about 150 miles to the south.

CHRISTY

Well, fine weather be after him, (*going to* MICHAEL, *coaxingly*)
and I'm thinking you wouldn't wish to have that quaking   395
blackguard in your house at all. Let you give us your blessing
and hear her swear her faith to me, for I'm mounted on the
⟋ spring-tide of the stars of luck, the way it'll be good for any
to have me in the house.

PEGEEN (*at the other side of* MICHAEL)

Bless us now, for I swear to God I'll wed him, and I'll not   400
renege.

MICHAEL (*standing up in the centre, holding on to both of them*)

It's the will of God, I'm thinking, that all should win an easy
or a cruel end, and it's the will of God that all should rear up
lengthy families for the nurture of the earth. What's a single
man, I ask you, eating a bit in one house and drinking a   405
sup in another, and he with no place of his own, like an old
braying jackass strayed upon the rocks? (*To* CHRISTY) It's
many would be in dread to bring your like into their house
for to end them, maybe, with a sudden end; but I'm a decent
man of Ireland, and I liefer face the grave untimely and I   410
seeing a score of grandsons growing up little gallant
swearers by the name of God, than go peopling my bedside
with puny weeds the like of what you'd breed, I'm thinking,
out of Shaneen Keogh. (*He joins their hands*) A daring fellow
is the jewel of the world, and a man did split his father's   415
middle with a single clout, should have the bravery of ten,
so may God and Mary and St. Patrick bless you, and increase
you from this mortal day.

CHRISTY *and* PEGEEN

Amen, O Lord!

> *Hubbub outside. Old* MAHON *rushes in, followed by all the*
> *crowd, and* WIDOW QUIN. *He makes a rush at* CHRISTY,
> *knocks him down, and begins to beat him*

414–15 *fellow is the* Maunsel (fellow, the TS, P)

PEGEEN (*dragging back his arm*)

    Stop that, will you. Who are you at all?   420

MAHON

    His father, God forgive me!

PEGEEN (*drawing back*)

    Is it rose from the dead?

MAHON

    Do you think I look so easy quenched with the tap of a loy?

                                      Beats CHRISTY *again*

PEGEEN (*glaring at* CHRISTY)

    And it's lies you told, letting on you had him slitted, and you
    nothing at all.   425

CHRISTY (*catching* MAHON's *stick*)

    He's not my father. He's a raving maniac would scare the
    world. (*Pointing to* WIDOW QUIN) Herself knows it is true.

CROWD

    You're fooling Pegeen! The Widow Quin seen him this day,
    and you likely knew! You're a liar!

CHRISTY (*dumbfounded*)

    It's himself was a liar, lying stretched out with an open head   430
    on him, letting on he was dead.

MAHON

    Weren't you off racing the hills before I got my breath with
    the start I had seeing you turn on me at all?

PEGEEN

    And to think of the coaxing glory we had given him, and he
    after doing nothing but hitting a soft blow and chasing   435
    northward in a sweat of fear. Quit off from this.

CHRISTY (*piteously*)

    You've seen my doings this day, and let you save me from the
    old man; for why would you be in such a scorch of haste to
    spur me to destruction now?

PEGEEN

    It's there your treachery is spurring me, till I'm hard set to   440
    think you're the one I'm after lacing in my heart-strings
    half-an-hour gone by. (*To* MAHON) Take him on from this,

for I think bad the world should see me raging for a Munster
liar, and the fool of men.

MAHON

Rise up now to retribution, and come on with me. 445

CROWD (*jeeringly*)

There's the playboy! There's the lad thought he'd rule the
roost in Mayo. Slate him now, mister.

CHRISTY (*getting up in shy terror*)

What is it drives you to torment me here, when I'd ask the
thunders of the might of God to blast me if I ever did hurt
to any saving only that one single blow. 450

MAHON (*loudly*)

If you didn't, you're a poor good-for-nothing, and isn't it
by the like of you the sins of the whole world are committed?

CHRISTY (*raising his hands*)

In the name of the Almighty God . . .

MAHON

Leave troubling the Lord God. Would you have him sending
down droughts, and fevers, and the old hen and the cholera 455
morbus?

CHRISTY (*to* WIDOW QUIN)

Will you come between us and protect me now?

WIDOW QUIN

I've tried a lot, God help me, and my share is done.

CHRISTY (*looking round in desperation*)

And I must go back unto my torment is it, or run off like a
vagabond straying through the Unions with the dusts of 460
August making mudstains in the gullet of my throat, or the

---

448 *I'd ask* (ed. following Quinn) (I'd asked TS, P, Maunsel)
459 *unto* Quinn, TS (into P, Maunsel)

---

447 *Slate* beat unmercifully.
455 *old hen* influenza (*Works*, II, 61).
455-6 *cholera morbus* possibly with the popular meaning of Asiatic cholera.
The 'choler' was described to Synge by an old man as one of the three
plagues of Ireland, the others being the great wind (1839) and the
Great Famine (*Works*, II, 213-14).

winds of March blowing on me till I'd take an oath I felt
them making whistles of my ribs within?

SARA

Ask Pegeen to aid you. Her like does often change.

CHRISTY

I will not then, for there's torment in the splendour of 465
her like, and she a girl any moon of midnight would take
pride to meet, facing southwards on the heaths of Keel.
But what did I want crawling forward to scorch my understanding at her flaming brow?

PEGEEN (*to* MAHON, *vehemently, fearing she will break into tears*)

Take him on from this or I'll set the young lads to destroy 470
him here.

MAHON (*going to him, shaking his stick*)

Come on now if you wouldn't have the company to see you
skelped.

PEGEEN (*half laughing, through her tears*)

That's it, now the world will see him pandied, and he an ugly
liar was playing off the hero, and the fright of men. 475

CHRISTY (*to* MAHON, *very sharply*)

Leave me go!

CROWD

That's it. Now Christy. If them two set fighting, it will lick
the world.

MAHON (*making a grab at* CHRISTY)

Come here to me.

CHRISTY (*more threateningly*)

Leave me go, I'm saying. 480

MAHON

I will maybe, when your legs is limping, and your back is
blue.

CROWD

Keep it up the two of you. I'll back the old one. Now the
playboy.

---

474 *pandied* beaten.

CHRISTY (*in a low and intense voice*)

Shut your yelling, for if you're after making a mighty man of　485
me this day by the power of a lie, you're setting me now to
think if it's a poor thing to be lonesome, it's worse maybe
to go mixing with the fools of earth.

　　　　　　　　　　　MAHON *makes a movement towards him*

CHRISTY (*almost shouting*)

Keep off . . . lest I do show a blow unto the lot of you would
set the guardian angels winking in the clouds above.　490

　　*He swings round with a sudden rapid movement and picks up
　　a loy*

CROWD (*half frightened, half amused*)

He's going mad! Mind yourselves! Run from the <u>idiot</u>!

CHRISTY

If I am an idiot, I'm after hearing my voice this day saying
words would raise the topknot on a poet in a merchant's
town. I've won your racing, and your lepping, and . . .

MAHON

Shut your gullet and come on with me.　495

CHRISTY

I'm going, but I'll stretch you first.

　　He runs at old MAHON *with the loy, chases him out of the
　　door, followed by* CROWD *and* WIDOW QUIN. *There is a great
　　noise outside, then a yell, and dead silence for a moment.*
　　CHRISTY *comes in, half dazed, and goes to fire*

WIDOW QUIN (*coming in, hurriedly, and going to him*)

They're turning again you. Come on, or you'll be hanged,
indeed.

CHRISTY

I'm thinking, from this out, Pegeen'll be giving me praises,
the same as in the hours gone by.　500

WIDOW QUIN (*impatiently*)

Come by the back-door. I'd think bad to have you stifled on
the gallows tree.

488 *to go* Quinn, TS (go P, Maunsel)

CHRISTY (*indignantly*)

I will not, then. What good'd be my life-time, if I left Pegeen?

WIDOW QUIN

Come on, and you'll be no worse than you were last night;
and you with a double murder this time to be telling to the   505
girls.

CHRISTY

I'll not leave Pegeen Mike.

WIDOW QUIN (*impatiently*)

Isn't there the match of her in every parish public, from
Binghamstown unto the plain of Meath? Come on, I tell you,
and I'll find you finer sweethearts at each waning moon.   510

CHRISTY

It's Pegeen I'm seeking only, and what'd I care if you
brought me a drift of chosen females, standing in their shifts
itself, maybe, from this place to the Eastern World?

SARA (*runs in, pulling off one of her petticoats*)

They're going to hang him. (*Holding out petticoat and shawl*)
Fit these upon him, and let him run off to the east.   515

WIDOW QUIN

He's raving now; but we'll fit them on him, and I'll take
him, in the ferry, to the Achill boat.

CHRISTY (*struggling feebly*)

Leave me go, will you? when I'm thinking of my luck today, for
she will wed me surely, and I a proven hero in the end of all.

They try to fasten petticoat round him

519 s.d. *They try to fasten* Maunsel (They fasten TS, P)

---

509 *Binghamstown . . . Meath* the breadth of Ireland, 'from this place to the
Eastern World'.

512 *shifts* the notorious obscene word to which Dublin objected. Anti-
Parnellites had used a shift as a symbol for Kitty O'Shea, Parnell's
mistress and later (June 1891) his wife (Herbert Howarth, *The Irish
Writers*, 1958, p. 231).

517 *Achill* an island a short way to the south, where Keel is located. It was
here that Lynchehaun was sheltered.

WIDOW QUIN

Take his left hand, and we'll pull him now. Come on, young   520
fellow.

CHRISTY (*suddenly starting up*)

You'll be taking me from her? You're jealous, is it, of her
wedding me? Go on from this.

> *He snatches up a stool, and threatens them with it*

WIDOW QUIN (*going*)

It's in the mad-house they should put him, not in jail, at all.
We'll go by the back-door, to call the doctor, and we'll save   525
him so.

> *She goes out, with* SARA, *through inner room.* MEN *crowd in
> the doorway.* CHRISTY *sits down again by the fire*

MICHAEL (*in a terrified whisper*)

Is the old lad killed surely?

PHILLY

I'm after feeling the last gasps quitting his heart.

> *They peer in at* CHRISTY

MICHAEL (*with a rope*)

Look at the way he is. Twist a hangman's knot on it, and
slip it over his head, while he's not minding at all.   530

PHILLY

Let you take it, Shaneen. You're the soberest of all that's
here.

SHAWN

Is it me to go near him, and he the wickedest and worst with
me? Let you take it, Pegeen Mike.

PEGEEN

Come on, so.   535

> *She goes forward with the others, and they drop the double
> hitch over his head*

---

526 s.d. *fire* Maunsel (fire taking off petticoat TS)
527 *the old lad* Maunsel (he TS)
535 s.d. *double hitch* Maunsel (loop TS)

CHRISTY

What ails you?

SHAWN (*triumphantly, as they pull the rope tight on his arms*)

Come on to the peelers, till they stretch you now.

CHRISTY

Me!

MICHAEL

If we took pity on you, the Lord God would, maybe, bring us
ruin from the law today, so you'd best come easy, for hanging   540
is an easy and a speedy end.

CHRISTY

I'll not stir. (*To* PEGEEN) And what is it you'll say to me, and
I after doing it this time in the face of all?

PEGEEN

I'll say, a strange man is a marvel, with his mighty talk;
but what's a squabble in your back-yard, and the blow of a   545
loy, have taught me that there's a great gap between a
gallous story and a dirty deed. (*To* MEN) Take him on from
this, or the lot of us will be likely put on trial for his deed
today.

CHRISTY (*with horror in his voice*)

And it's yourself will send me off, to have a horny-fingered   550
hangman hitching his bloody slip-knots at the butt of my ear.

MEN (*pulling rope*)

Come on, will you?

He is pulled down on the floor

CHRISTY (*twisting his legs round the table*)

Cut the rope, Pegeen, and I'll quit the lot of you, and live
from this out, like the madmen of Keel, eating muck and
green weeds, on the faces of the cliffs.   555

PEGEEN

And leave us to hang, is it, for a saucy liar, the like of you?
(*To* MEN) Take him on, out from this.

557 *on, out* Maunsel (on TS)

SHAWN

Pull a twist on his neck, and squeeze him so.

PHILLY

Twist yourself. Sure he cannot hurt you, if you keep your
distance from his teeth alone.   560

SHAWN

I'm afeard of him. (*To* PEGEEN) Lift a lighted sod, will
you, and scorch his leg.

PEGEEN (*blowing the fire with a bellows*)

Leave go now, young fellow, or I'll scorch your shins.

CHRISTY

You're blowing for to torture me? (*His voice rising and
growing stronger*) That's your kind, is it? Then let the   565
lot of you be wary, for, if I've to face the gallows, I'll
have a gay march down, I tell you, and shed the blood of
some of you before I die.

SHAWN (*in terror*)

Keep a good hold, Philly. Be wary, for the love of God.
For I'm thinking he would liefest wreak his pains on me.   570

CHRISTY (*almost gaily*)

If I do lay my hands on you, it's the way you'll be at the
fall of night, hanging as a scarecrow for the fowls of hell.
Ah, you'll have a gallous jaunt I'm saying, coaching out
through Limbo with my father's ghost.

SHAWN (*to* PEGEEN)

Make haste, will you? Oh, isn't he a holy terror, and isn't it 575
true for Father Reilly, that all drink's a curse that has the
lot of you so shaky and uncertain now?

CHRISTY

If I can wring a neck among you, I'll have a royal judgement
looking on the trembling jury in the courts of law. And
won't there be crying out in Mayo the day I'm stretched   580
upon the rope, with ladies in their silks and satins snivelling
in their lacy kerchiefs, and they rhyming songs and ballads
on the terror of my fate.

   He squirms round on the floor and bites SHAWN's *leg*

SHAWN (*shrieking*)

My leg's bit on me! He's the like of a mad dog, I'm thinking, the way that I will surely die. 585

CHRISTY (*delighted with himself*)

You will then, the way you can shake out hell's flags of welcome for my coming in two weeks or three, for I'm thinking Satan hasn't many have killed their da in Kerry, and in Mayo too.

Old MAHON *comes in behind on all fours and looks on unnoticed*

MEN (*to* PEGEEN)

Bring the sod, will you. 590

PEGEEN (*coming over*)

God help him so. (*Burns his leg*)

CHRISTY (*kicking and screaming*)

Oh, glory be to God!

He kicks loose from the table, and they all drag him towards the door

JIMMY (*seeing old* MAHON)

Will you look what's come in?

They all drop CHRISTY *and run left*

CHRISTY (*scrambling on his knees face to face with old* MAHON)

Are you coming to be killed a third time, or what ails you now? 595

MAHON

For what is it they have you tied?

CHRISTY

They're taking me to the peelers to have me hanged for slaying you.

MICHAEL (*apologetically*)

It is the will of God that all should guard their little cabins from the treachery of law, and what would my daughter be 600 doing if I was ruined or was hanged itse'f?

---

589 s.d. *on unnoticed* Maunsel (on TS)

MAHON (*grimly, loosening* CHRISTY)

It's little I care if you put a bag on her back, and went
picking cockles till the hour of death; but my son and myself
will be going our own way, and we'll have great times from
this out telling stories of the villainy of Mayo, and the fools   605
is here. (*To* CHRISTY, *who is freed*) Come on now.

CHRISTY

Go with you, is it? I will then, like a gallant captain with
his heathen slave. Go on now and I'll see you from this day
stewing my oatmeal and washing my spuds, for I'm master of
all fights from now. (*Pushing* MAHON) Go on, I'm saying.   610

MAHON

Is it me?

CHRISTY

Not a word out of you. Go on from this.

MAHON (*walking out and looking back at* CHRISTY *over his
shoulder*)

Glory be to God! (*With a broad smile*) I am crazy again!

Goes

CHRISTY

Ten thousand blessings upon all that's here, for you've
turned me a likely gaffer in the end of all, the way I'll go   615
romancing through a romping lifetime from this hour to the
dawning of the judgement day.

He goes out

MICHAEL

By the will of God, we'll have peace now for our drinks.
Will you draw the porter, Pegeen?

SHAWN (*going up to her*)

It's a miracle Father Reilly can wed us in the end of all,   620
and we'll have none to trouble us when his vicious bite is
healed.

616 *a romping* Maunsel (my romping TS)

PEGEEN (*hitting him a box on the ear*)
    Quit my sight. (*Putting her shawl over her head and breaking
    out into wild lamentations*) Oh my grief, I've lost him
    surely. I've lost the only playboy of the Western World.   625

CURTAIN

624–5 *I've lost . . . I've lost* Maunsel (I lost . . . I have lost TS)

---

624 *Oh my grief* A conventional formula to introduce a lament in Lady
    Gregory's and Douglas Hyde's translations. On the first night the keen
    counterpointed that which ends *Riders to the Sea* which opened the bill.

APPENDIX

JOHN McGOLDRICK AND THE QUAKER'S DAUGHTER

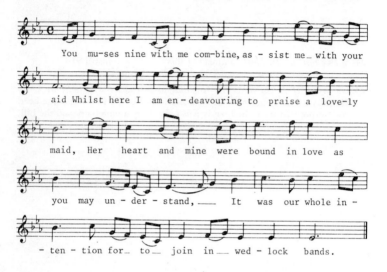

You mu-ses nine with me com-bine, as-sist me with your aid Whilst here I am en-deavouring to praise a love-ly maid, Her heart and mine were bound in love as you may un-der-stand, ___ It was our whole in--ten-tion for_ to_ join in_ wed-lock bands.

I hope you'll pay attention, and the truth to you I'll tell;
She was a Quaker's daughter, a maid I loved right well.
We being not of one persuasion, her father made a plan,
He done his whole endeavour to hang me in the wrong.

My name is John McGoldrick, the same I'll ne'er deny –
They swore I was a radical; condemned I was to die.
As soon as my dead letter came, my sorrows did renew,
Saying, 'For to die I do deny – Brave boys, what shall I do?'

At length my dearest jewel became servant in the jail;
She found her opportunity and did it not conceal.
She says, 'Young John McGoldrick, I hope to be your wife;
I will do my best endeavour to save your precious life.'

That night the god of Bacchus to the jailer did appear,
All with a club of gentlemen inviting him to beer.
They had the strongest liquor and the very best of wine –
The jailer and the turnkey to sleep they did incline.

She says, 'Young John McGoldrick, I hope you will agree.
And bind yourself upon your oath, and come along with me;
For I have stole the jailer's keys, and I could do no more,'
That very night I took my flight out of the prison door.

Early the next morning the hurry it begun,
The 66th pursued us without either fife or drum.
The jailer and the turnkey they quickly ran us down,
And brought us back as prisoners once more to Cavan town.

And there we lay bewailing, all in a prison bound,
With heavy bolts of iron secured unto the ground.
All for a second trial they brought us to the jail;
Their intention was to hang me, and send her to New South
    Wales.

But I may thank Lord Corry, and his father, Lord Belmore
Long may they live in splendour around Loch Erne shore!
They sent me a grand character, as plainly you may see,
Which caused the judge and jury that day to set us free.

You reader, now excuse me, I did refine my quill,
The praises of a lovely maid these papers for to fill.
For I have become her husband, and she my loving wife;
In spite of her old father, she saved my precious life.

Printed in Great Britain by
The Garden City Press Limited
Letchworth, Hertfordshire
SG6 1JS